A Symposium on

Christian Reconstruction,

Family Business, and Dominion

RECONSTRUCTION LIFE

Reconstruction Life
2458 Lake Forest Drive
Oak Harbor, WA 98277
Email: admin@reconstructionlife.com
Website: reconstructionlife.com

Cover Design: Jessica Graham
Imprint: Independently Published by Reconstruction Life
Printed in the United States of America

ISBN 13: 978-1093613971

A Symposium on

Christian Reconstruction,

Family Business, and Dominion

Reconstructing Our Lives, Families, and Assets toward Godly

Dominion and Generational Stability in the Marketplace

Joseph M Graham—Editor-in-Chief

Symposium on Christian Reconstruction

Acknowledgements

Many families and individuals helped bring together this symposium. We are extremely grateful for the contributions of our keynote speakers, Mark Rushdoony, Tim Yarbrough and Michael Kloss, for the contributions of the local workshop speakers, and for the help of Jason Diffner and Daniel Eby in planning this symposium.

For all their many efforts both at the event and especially for bearing the preponderance of duties for compiling and editing this book we are appreciative of Dan and Susan Eby. They are faithful servants of the Lord who are a tremendous blessing to all of us in the Pacific Northwest.

Symposium on Christian Reconstruction

Table of Contents

Introduction

By Joseph M. Graham

Welcome to the Mountain!

The deep valleys in the Cascade mountains reminded me of something I couldn't quite place.

Our 2nd Annual Pacific Northwest Christian Reconstruction Conference is nestled in two deep valleys at the Tall Timber Ranch outside beautiful Leavenworth, WA. I'd never been to this location before, but the shape and lay of the land reminded me of something familiar, but what?

The first morning of our conference, out of the blue, a loud ripping roar came through the valley bringing everyone to a halt. I caught a glimpse of a fighter jet roaring through the valley, banking around the mountains. It was then that I realized why I remembered this place. Our host sits directly under the "Whidbey H," a famous location to all the fighter pilots from Whidbey Island, marking the last landmark on route to the climax of the most magnificent low-level route in the United States: VR-1355. I have footage of this valley from the cockpit of my Growler ripping through the mountains en route to the summit of Glacier Peak.

Those who have flown the route smile while reminiscing about the experience. Little did those pilots realize on that crisp morning they had historically opened the first

1

Symposium on Christian Reconstruction Family Business conference in our region.

Approximately 100 individuals gathered one early June weekend to learn about family business and the importance of the subject in Christian thought. Many Reconstructionists and others curious about a Christian family business conference came together to seek wisdom and guidance from the dozens of speakers in attendance. Our speakers come from the presuppositional, covenantal, and optimistic outlook which characterizes Reconstructionists. What these families enjoyed was a gathering of minds devoted to an all-encompassing orthodoxy that seeks an unstoppable application to Christian living.

My family has lived in the Pacific Northwest on Whidbey Island since 2011. I arrived here for initial flight training as an EA-18G Growler pilot with the US Navy. We have lived here ever since. My wife and I, over the past ten years, have been led to the conviction that Christians have a duty to be a part of the cultural growth and advocacy of Christ's Kingdom. We've been inspired to advance the comprehensive principles of God's Word and Law in every sphere of life within our own family, and to be ambassadors for the same in others.

We desire to explain the principles and convictions of comprehensive Christian thought with those who are unfamiliar, and fellowship with others already convinced of the same. This event allows those in our region the opportunity to discuss these theological foundations from a covenantal, theonomic, and postmillennial perspective– those who are talking about and sharing the many implications and principles in thought and life.

Having a regional conference allows us the opportunity to share and discuss with other great thinking, intentional, deeply-committed, and principled families and individuals about the vast implications of Christian fundamentals. Our proximity also allows us the opportunity of fellowship to grow closer together and co-labor regularly.

The Christian Reconstruction of Family Business conference centered around the recognition and development of the tools of dominion that God has given families related to the marketplace. We desire to cultivate our God-given assets toward generational stability in the marketplace, anchoring the fact that we each are given talents and abilities from the Lord. These tools are meant to be honed in the marketplace and used for production multi-generationally.

Why Do We Gather Here?

"Who is the man who fears the LORD?
Him will he instruct in the way that he should choose.
His soul shall abide in well-being,
and his offspring shall inherit the land."
Psalm 25:12-13

For the family that aspires to achieve a productive family business, the appropriate starting point is the fear of the Lord. As the psalmist describes, there is solace for the man with the proper fear of the Lord. With such, the family of God has all the tools necessary to achieve a vibrant, profitable family enterprise the lasts through generations.

Prosperity is possible because of the source of wisdom and discernment. The man who fears the Lord can be both entrepreneurial and have a soul at rest, an incredibly valuable commodity. The price tag on such a Pro-Commodity is inconceivable, with all of the challenges and difficulties intrinsic in running a business. The fact is that the instruction that comes from the Lord's guidance is an incredible source of business capital.

3

This verse provides a constant source of solace for the multi-generational family business. The great hope we have in industry, under the proper fear of the Lord, will be a long-lasting and enduring source of increase for ours and many other families for generations to come. The pinnacle of achievement for a family business, with the proper vision and foundations, is becoming productive, and providing value for ages.

When we engage in the marketplace, it can be difficult to make choices as to which field to pursue. Which associates should we employ? How does the prospect of a family enterprise impact or change our family dynamics? These critical concerns and questions are precisely why an event like the Christian Reconstruction of Family Business Conference is so needed and valuable.

Our Groundings

The foundational principles that we gather around are what allow us to move forward from belief to action. The ideas that were grounding our event begin with a belief in the sufficiency of scripture.

The word of God is more than infallible and inerrant; it is authoritative on everything about which it speaks, and it speaks about everything. We believe that the Bible is perfect (Ps. 19:7), inerrant (Prov. 30:5-6), and complete (2 Tim. 3:16, 17), therefore it applies to every situation which we encounter. Furthermore, the authority which the Bible possesses is not restricted to "spiritual," "heavenly," personal or inward issues. As Dr. Joseph Moorecraft states in his book *Authentic Christianity:*

> "Its authority is life-wide and comprehensive. It gives infallible direction on issues covering the whole range of human experience. It informs politics (Rom. 13:1f),

jurisprudence (Deut. 16:18f), the military and warfare (Deut. 20:1f), loans and interest (Ex. 22:25f); marriage (Eph. 5:22f), education (Deut. 6:1f); ethics (Lev. 19:1f), crime and punishment (Lev. 20:1f), labor and management (Deut. 24:14f), funerals (Deut. 14:1f), inflation (Is. 1:22), ecology and environmental concerns (Deut. 22:1f); agriculture (Deut. 22:6f), divorce (Matt. 5:31f), free enterprise (Deut. 28:1f), worship (Ps. 84:1f), property rights (Deut. 19:14f), church discipline (Matt. 18:15f), art and music (2 Chron. 3:16; Ps. 98:5), and culture in all its aspects (Gen. 1:28f)."

The belief in the sufficiency of scripture is an all-encompassing belief that anchors the mind and soul in the word of God. We couldn't possibly begin to discuss the implications of a business endeavor without this grounding.

We also affirm the totality of scripture as a necessary belief. The Bible in its 66 books, as Old and New Testament, provides us with a sufficient body of truth that contains all that man needs to know about God's explanation of Himself, man and creation (John 17:17; Ps. 119:160). He provides us with a perfect gospel for all men and all time, with unchangeable promises. The Bible provides us with perfect truth and instruction that addresses every problem or conflict that could ever be encountered (1 Cor. 10:13).

Since the Lord Jesus Christ is the same yesterday, today and forever, we can rest assured that upon all that we hope and rest is the same as the saints before or after us. As the called out ones of God we have the distinct responsibility for governing, serving, teaching, laboring, and producing.

Our event is not unique, but in some respects it is. We know that there is nothing new under the sun. There is nothing that we encounter or face that hasn't existed in ages past, nor is there any decision that hasn't been faced by men or women in times before. This provides us with tremendous hope because we have the words of God, which are imminently sufficient and practical for our lives. The Word will always be relevant. It will always be applicable. It will always have guidance about how we should proceed in our life.

The second Pacific Northwest Christian Reconstruction Conference is only the vehicle for our assembling. As a vehicle, it is entirely inconsequential, but as regards our mission– applying the Word of God to every area of life– it is fundamental. I strongly encourage each region of our Lord's Kingdom to gather as best suits them, to address the idolatry of our day. We in the Pacific Northwest stand with you.

Many Thanks

Thank you to all of the speakers who provided valuable insight and contributions to this event. I am very grateful for their contributions. Unfortunately, every topic that was addressed at this event didn't make it into this published book. This absence is because some issues were better suited to a live presentation.

It is our hope that as these annual events continue, we will have the companion book printed and ready for distribution before the start of the conference.

Thank you to all the volunteers who helped make this event and publication a success. Many hands and prayers were involved in the work.

We are already preparing for our 2019 event at Tall Timber Lodge on September 6 to 8, 2019. This year's theme will be: *A Symposium on Biblical Law and Christian Education*, which we expect to be just as valuable and profitable.

I hope this book is a blessing to you and I pray we see you in the Pacific Northwest soon!

Joseph M. Graham
Reconstruction Life
Joseph.Matthew.Graham@gmail.com

Part I

An Introduction to

Christian Reconstruction

The Origins of Christian Reconstruction

Mark R. Rushdoony

"Christian Reconstruction" is a relatively recent term, though it is not a new idea. My father coined the term in 1965 in his second Newsletter which later came to be called the Chalcedon Report. In the first newsletter, he had compared the work he envisioned ahead as a "Christian Renaissance." In the second issue dated October 31,1965, he used another analogy.

During this past month in the course of my travels, I spent several hours visiting with an outstanding conservative leader, a man who is a major force in one of our most notable anti-communist organizations. In the first few minutes, he raised the question, "Do you see any hope?" Many ask this same question.

I am reminded of the question asked of Adoniram Judson (1788-1850), pioneer American Baptist missionary in Burma. Hostile forces soon succeeded in destroying Judson's mission, his converts, printing press, and his possessions. Judson himself was thrown into a filthy Burmese prison, and with arrogant humor, he was asked by a captor, "How are your prospects now?" "As bright as the promises of God!" responded Judson, who lived to see those promises fulfilled in the success of his mission. Our prospects are also as bright, if our confidence is in the same omnipotent God.

The revolution of our day rests on certain anti-Christian premises:

First, it is held that "anything goes," because there is no God. No God means no law, and no law means that nothing is a crime, and hence all acts are equally valid.

Second, by outlawing God and declaring Him to be non-existent, the revolutionaries outlaw the idea of good and evil. They are supposedly *beyond* good and evil. If good is mythical, then evil is also, and man cannot be evil! Therefore, whatever the world-planners do cannot be evil, because evil does not exist– it is simply either a successful scientific experiment, or it is a failure.

Third, because God is abolished as a myth, the approach to man's problems must be scientific– that is, experimental– and man is thus the prime laboratory test animal. In school, your children are to be objects of experimentation, even as you are also, by means of every communication media. There is no evil in such experimentation since there is no God, but only success or failure.

Fourth, every experiment, to be valid, requires total control of all factors. Hence, the scientific society must be totalitarian to the full measure, or it will not work.
The various phases of this vast attempt to turn the world from God's creation to the scientific planners' re-creation can be documented in detail. It has been done by the volume. The answer, however, is not in facts and knowledge, but in a restoration of Christian faith.

Because God is God, and because He will not allow Himself to be dethroned, the scientific planners are doomed. This judgment is a certainty because God cannot allow sin to go unpunished. All sin is either atoned for, or punished. The question is whether we will be among those judged, or among those– the saved remnant– who shall undertake even now the task of reconstruction.

Thus was the term "Christian Reconstruction" born. The term is really no more than an analogy which pictures the work and responsibility of Christians as citizens of the Kingdom of God. It is the teaching commandment of the Great Commission. The message of Christian Reconstruction is that our problems are caused by sin, and that the only way of blessing is a self-conscious obedience.

Rebellion against God never works, so man's problems will progress towards systemic failure. In one area after another, modern man has rebelled against God, so we are increasingly seeing the approach of system failures. The alternative is to rethink our institutions and actions, and rebuild or reconstruct them on the Word of God. We start by changing ourselves and our families, then move to our vocations, and our larger sphere of influence.

Our concern here is to explore why it was that my father felt the urgency to present this concept to the church in 1965. It was not because he felt it would be readily accepted! Rather, he saw it as a long-term necessity because our culture was moving toward a systemic failure, and some idea had to be in place and at work on a grassroots level that would be an alternative when modern culture was wracked by failures. Our proximity to those failures is now far more apparent than in 1965!

The Bible gives us a "big picture" view of all of history. It begins with God's decrees before the Creation, and ends with a glimpse of the eternal Kingdom so that we can put our own lives and responsibilities into a larger context. Christian Reconstruction is an analogy on how we go about that. It presumes there is a problem, some structure that is failing that needs rebuilt. My father originated this term, and

I can give some historical insight into his thinking, so that is what I will focus on.

Armenian Roots

My father was conceived in the Old World and born in the New. The family had lived in ancient Armenia for millennia, but was displaced by the genocide of Armenians that began in 1915.

The name "Rushdoony" has as its root "Rush" or "Rusa." The name means "the house or dynasty of Rusa."

This root "Rusa" was also my father's given name, and goes back to the last dynasty of the Kingdom of Urartu from which our family descends. Urartu is the Assyrian name for Ararat. When the authorized version refers to Armenia, it is giving a slightly later historic name, so it would be more accurate to say "the Kingdom of Ararat" or Urartu. The Kingdom of Urartu harassed its southern neighbor Assyria for centuries. The latter could not move south toward Jerusalem because of the threat of Urartu to the north. Every time Assyria moved south, the Urartans would take the opportunity to move southward and cut off the east-west trade routes which brought wealth to Assyria. This was one reason Assyria never conquered Jerusalem, as it had Samaria.

After the end of the Urartan era, the Armenian era began, which was less centralized and less warlike. Though their name devised from the Urartan kings, the Rushdoonys became a prominent ruling family near Van, the ancient center of the Urartan Empire. A portion of the Van district was named after the Rushdoonys.

Centuries later, the Armenian nation was the first to officially adopt Christianity. The Rushdoonys became a prominent

14

line of priests, as it early became a custom for prominent families to sponsor a priest. In the tenth century, there were several Rushdoonys who served as the "catholicos" or head of the Armenian church. The Armenian church has always been independent. If you have been to Jerusalem, you have noted that one of the "quarters" of the old city is the Armenian, controlled by the Armenian church.

There were six generations of father-son priests prior to my grandfather's exposure to Presbyterianism in the late nineteenth century. His father was blinded, then killed by Turks. Shortly thereafter, his mother and siblings died, and he was left an orphan. He was sick, so his extended family took him to the Presbyterian orphanage and mission hospital at Van. He regained his health, and because he was so bright, his extended family was urged to leave him there to be educated.

Later, the mission enabled my grandfather's college education in Turkey, and then his post-graduate degree at the University of Edinburgh. After graduating, my grandfather returned to the mission at Van to work, and married my grandmother. Soon a son was born, named Rousas George.

The Armenians, being Christian in the Muslim Ottoman Empire (now Turkey), were often the victims of violence, theft, and discrimination. Several periods of violence occurred in the late 19th and early years of the 20th century. During WWI, while other nations were too preoccupied to interfere, Turkey decided to eliminate its Christian Armenian population. About 1½ million died by direct means, or during forced marches.

The city of Van was unique in that it had the highest concentration of Armenians in the Ottoman Empire. When word of the massacres got to Van, they were able to throw up two improvised defensive positions, one in the old Armenian quarters and a second around the American

Presbyterian mission. This became known as "the Defense of Van." Unable to overcome either position, the Turkish military withdrew, but not before Rousas George died of illness that had swept through the crowded conditions.

The Russian army then moved south and camped at Van during the summer of 1915 when my father was conceived. That fall, events changed rapidly. The war did not go well for the Russians (a fact later used by the Bolsheviks to overthrow the Czar). Their sudden announcement of their withdrawal to Russia, a hundred miles to the north, caused a mass exodus from Van. Those who stayed faced the certain wrath of the Turkish forces.

By a series of providential events, my grandparents made it to Russia and were allowed to immediately leave Archangel for New York City. Their American sponsor was Dr. George Raynolds, who had founded the American mission in Van. My father was born five months later, at which time the family traveled to Kingsburg, California where my grandfather had been called as the founding pastor of Armenian Martyrs Presbyterian Church.

I recount this lengthy background because it was never far from my father's thinking. My father's upbringing was very Armenian. He did not speak much English before he started school, and his home church was Armenian-speaking. Some of his earliest recollections were of Armenian visitors to the farm. They would typically inquire if my grandfather had heard any word of this relative or that. Sometimes very grim accounts were related.

My father grew up with a very keen awareness of the fact that the Armenian people had been massacred or run out of their ancient homeland because they were Christians in a Muslim empire. Frequently the family would observe fasts for the starving Armenians trapped in Russia through its communist revolution and the famine of the early 1920's.

Many years later, my mother made an observation about my father that was very true. Because he knew, understood, and appreciated the Christian faith that had been instrumental in defining both Armenians and Americans, she said my father was more American than most Americans, and more Armenian than most Armenians.

My father once recounted the distress of some of the Armenian immigrants later in life. In the 1950's they were discussing the changes they were seeing in America, and made what to them was a damning statement, that America was becoming another Turkey. The Armenian experience was never far removed from my father's thinking. In it, he saw the contempt with which Christianity would be treated by other religions.

That contempt against Christianity grew throughout the twentieth century. It was evident in the Scopes trial of 1925 in which those Christians who refused to profess evolution were labeled "ignoramuses" by Clarence Darrow. It was evident in the changing morals of the 1950's and 1960's. My father's family history allowed him to see that the end result of non-Christian rule would be an intense hostility toward Christianity.

The University Years

My father graduated from the University of California at Berkeley, earning a BA in English in 1938 and an MA in Education in 1940. This was during the Depression and before the Cold War, when Marxism was openly avowed. In 1934, right out of high school, my father had gotten his first exposure to Marxism. He had moved to San Francisco where my grandfather was pastoring a church. His first job was working 59 hours a week for $14, a position that was highly coveted by older men at the time. That job ended abruptly when the Marxist Harry Bridges organized a general strike, one accompanied by no small amount of violence.

There was no self-conscious Christian worldview thinking at the time. My father's own intellectual history had little guidance. His voracious reading was a help, because it made him somewhat independent intellectually. He became suspicious of the university, and really came to hate it as a degenerate institution. He later admitted he had something of a rebellious attitude; he would often enroll in a class, then drop it when he became disillusioned with it.

Even his personal reading became a struggle. Churchmen he respected told him he needed to read the ancient classics to be a truly educated man. He began a systematic personal study of classical literature. He recalled it as one of the ugliest experiences of his life, as he was searching for the wisdom of the ages he had been assured was there, but came to realize these classics were not only devoid of wisdom, but were– as he later put it– "humanistic garbage." He would call them "...classics of depravity, classics of degenerate cultures. What they offer at their best is evil."

As a young man, he saw a changing culture, yet no real push-back from the church. On the contrary, the modernists were embracing the changes, and the most notable resistance seemed to be the Fundamentalist movement, which effectively retreated from engagement by reducing Christianity to its "fundamental" points of orthodoxy. Their fight for the faith was one to save the church from modernism, not to advance the full-orbed Word of God.

Anti-Statism

Two ideas did begin to develop in his thinking, both encouraged, inadvertently, by professors. One idea was the competition of the state for the role and authority of the church. It was in a course on Byzantine history by Ernst Kantorowicz in a class lecture on the iconoclastic controversy. Kantorowicz said the issue was not about the theological propriety of images in churches, but rather one of the real manifestations of the divine. The church claimed it was, in effect, the continuing incarnation of God, and the state said that the *emperor* was. The real issue was which human institution spoke with the authority of God.

The state emerged victorious in that conflict, and set the stage for the ongoing conflict of Western history, where the state sees its role as divine. That idea has since been secularized into the idea of the state's sovereignty, the belief that ultimate power and authority resides in the crown, or today in the "democratic" state apparatus. This, of course, proved to be a recipe for tyranny, and the state is now seen as having ultimate authority in every realm.

Much of my father's writings were against statism, and he wrote against statism in terms of its inherently religious claim, one aspect of man's desire to "be as gods, knowing good and evil" (Gen. 3:5). This humanism replaces the authority of God with the authority of man, and the greatest collective voice of men is the nation state– whether an absolute monarch or the administration of a "democratic" government.

The common characteristic of ancient regimes was that regardless of their political form, the state claimed absolute power. It was Christianity that developed the first push-back to these inherently religious claims to power. Liberty was a product of Christianity in the west. The decline of Christianity, with its ascription of absolute power and authority to God alone, has seen a corresponding decline in liberty, and a rise in statism.

My father early saw the issue of ultimate authority. If ultimate authority was in man, absolutism would result. If it was in the church, ecclesiastical absolutism would emerge, as the Reformers came to realize. It was only Christianity in the West that struggled for centuries to bring all men under law and limit their jurisdiction. The Reformation addressed that in its denial of Rome's authority. The Puritans in both the English Civil War and the Glorious Revolution declared that the king was subject to the law. The American Constitution was an effort to define the limited extent of government authority via delegated powers. My father recognized in that class discussion that claims to ultimate authority were religious claims to sovereignty, and repeated man's original sin– the desire to "be as gods" (Genesis 3:5).

Presuppositions

A second idea that took root in my father's thinking in his university days was presuppositionalism, though not by that term. Another professor, Edwin Strong, made an impression on him by a random emphatic comment he made in response to a student during a class discussion. Strong warned the student that just as Augustine would not debate the existence of God, he should never debate the origins of the universe, because it would involve a miracle comparable to creation by God. Strong urged arguing in terms of the given.

A few years later, when my father first read Van Til's *The New Modernism,* he was immediately excited because he was speaking of the importance of the given in terms of systematically Christian thought based on the sovereign Creator God and His Word. Van Til's name for the given was "presupposition."

Biblical Law

In 1940, my father began his seminary work at a
Congregational seminary, the Pacific School of Religion,
also in Berkeley. He chose not to go to a local Presbyterian
seminary because it was also liberal, but claimed to be
orthodox. He felt he might just as well go to an honestly and
openly liberal seminary. In addition, about a third of his
credits were earned at nearby Episcopalian and Unitarian
seminaries.

Once in seminary, the issue of Biblical Law arose, and my
father made some comments to the effect that he believed
the Bible spoke to all of life, and he spoke in defense of
Biblical Law. He later said he "got clobbered" for his
statements, and he realized all the weight of modern
Christian thinking was against him! He decided he would
keep quiet on the subject until he could study extensively
and be fully prepared when he did speak out. That would be
over twenty years later, when Chalcedon afforded him the
opportunity to engage in that study.

First Pastorate

My father graduated from seminary in 1944, and was
ordained in the Presbyterian Church, U.S.A (PCUSA). He
hoped to find a small pastorate that would allow him
adequate time to read and study. What he found was a
mission church to Paiute and Sheshone Indians on the Duck
Valley Reservation. He lived at Owyhee, Nevada, on the
Idaho-Nevada border, about 100 miles from Mountain
Home, Idaho to the north and Elko, Nevada, to the south.

It was a difficult first pastorate, but the reaction he received
from many was far more honest than any he would receive
in a typical white community. It was prescient of an attitude
that would be common in those communities somewhat

later. That reaction was this: Christianity was like bags of used clothing sent to the mission, another one of the white man's cast-offs. It was something he no longer wanted or practiced, and so he was offering it to the Indian.

In 2013, we published a book of essays my father wrote on his recollections of his years on the reservation. As we prepared the manuscript, my father's comments suggested the title, *The American Indian: A Standing Indictment Against Christianity and Statism in America.* It was an indictment against statism because the reservation system has been America's greatest experiment in socialism, one which took all the admirable characteristics of the Indian and destroyed them in a generation.

My father recounts a conversation he had with an Indian who had traveled around the country during the war, over a decade into the New Deal. He said the American desire for ease and security had become "reservation fever," and it would destroy the American people like it had his own. The reservation system was also an indictment against American Christianity because the churches supported the idea of reservations as they thought reservations might be a means to evangelize the Indians.

He spent eight and a half years on the reservation. The long, hard winters did give him some opportunity to study, but the deplorable social and economic conditions on the reservation gave him some hard, real life examples of a broken culture– lessons most Americans would not grapple with for some years to come.

It was obvious that there was no simple fix to the problems he saw, and so he could only turn to their most basic need, a new foundation based on the truth of God. There could be no pretense that things were not serious, so he could be frank about their needs. The exceptions to the social, moral, and economic ills of the reservation were, he noted, the

Christian Indians, some of whom were well-to-do ranchers, and of whom he spoke nearly fifty years later as some of the finest men he had ever known.

Cornelius Van Til

During his years on the reservation, my father began to travel and speak. During one such trip, he picked up a copy of a new book by Cornelius Van Til in a minister's home and began browsing in it. It was *The New Modernism* and the minister urged him to keep it. He immediately was attracted to Van Til's use of presuppositional thinking, and recognized it as the Christian alternative to Edwin Strong's "given." All men used presuppositional thinking, Van Til held, so it was essential to self-consciously predicate one's thinking on the authoritative revelation of God's Word.

When my father read a very critical mid-Western seminary journal review of *The New Modernism*, he wrote a long letter to the editor detailing the importance of Van Til's insights. His concluding words in that letter were:

> *"The question is this: is his analysis correct? I believe that it is, and before entering seminary and before reading Calvin, I became a Calvinist on these philosophical and historical grounds illuminated by Van Til.*
>
> *To begin where Barth and Brunner have done in the autonomous consciousness of man leads inevitably to the same subjectivity. God, and not man, is the given. The attempt of dialectical theology to bridge the gap between the given, autonomous consciousness and the yon-side of God and the world is an exciting struggle, but thus far it is simply a magnificent failure. I trust that you will correct the grave injustice done to this splendid and very important book."*

He also wrote Van Til a letter, and included a copy of his letter to the editor. This began a long and cordial relationship with Van Til. A decade later (1958) my father published his first book, *By What Standard?* It was an analysis of the importance of Van Til's thought. In the foreword he wrote:

> *"The sovereignty of the self-contained God is the key to every field in that only the God of Scripture makes all things possible and explicable, and is thus the basic premise not only of theology, but of philosophy, science, and indeed all knowledge. In that God is the Creator of all things, He is their only valid principle of interpretation, in that they derive both their existence and meaning from His creative act."*

My father saw Van Til's approach as the only consistent counter to the humanistic approach to knowledge that pervaded secular thought and much Christian theology. He regularly contrasted God's will with man's will, God's revealed Law with man's positive law, and theism with humanism.

As the years went on, it became apparent that my father's application of presuppositionalism went further than Van Til. My father freely acknowledged this. Van Til was a philosopher of religion (at Westminster Theological Seminary) and he limited himself to that narrow field. But my father saw the implications of a systematic presuppositionalism, an epistemological application of walking by faith rather than by the sight of human reason. He once summed up the implications of Van Til's position as "...if the Word of God means anything, it means everything."

Eschatology

My father's eschatology was not settled until almost a decade after his seminary years. As with other subjects, he wanted to study as much as he could and be able to defend, not just advocate, a position. He began by studying the most popular eschatology of the twentieth century, the pre-tribulation rapture dispensationalism popularized by the Scofield Reference Bible. He was never attracted to it, and actually felt revulsion toward it as more akin to a fairy tale than anything else.

He also studied amillennial thinking because so many Reformed authors of the twentieth century believed it. He did not find it an attractive position, and would later criticize it (particularly its mid-century manifestations) as a commitment to defeat and irrelevance that he saw as a retreat from the implications of the Great Commission and the Kingdom of God.

Through reading Lorraine Boethner and B. B. Warfield, then Henrickson's *More Than Conquerors,* and Roderick Campbell's *Israel and the Covenant*, he came to consider himself a post-millennialist in the years just before his writing period began.

Much preaching about eschatology finds a ready audience because it caters to a curiosity about the future. My father's eschatology never catered to curiosity. It was a context in which he understood and explained Christian duty. As a post-millennial, he believed in the progress of the Kingdom of God toward its complete success in time and history.

His Christian Reconstruction must be seen in this light. It represents an analogy of Christian duty in the service of the Kingdom. It is not about bringing in the Kingdom by human activity, but human activity that is faithful to the King and His Law-Word.

Resisting Modernism

An Indian reservation was a difficult first pastorate, but at least the line of conflict between Christian and non-Christian was a clear one. It was not so in my father's church denomination. The battle against modernism in the PCUSA was being slowly lost. As early as 1950 when he was elected moderator of the Nevada Presbytery, he noted there was an effort to run orthodox, evangelical men out of the church.

After eight and a half years, my father accepted a call to Trinity Presbyterian Church in Santa Cruz, California. This required him to change presbyteries and receive the approval of the one which represented that area of California. There was a great deal of hostility to the prospect of his joining the presbytery, and a concerted, vicious effort to block his acceptance was made in 1952 that narrowly failed. In 1958 he left the PCUSA and joined the Orthodox Presbyterian Church, a small denomination that had split off the Presbyterian Church some years earlier.

The change in denominations caused a change in his ministry. While a clergyman for the PCUSA, he spoke to numerous community and service organizations. He had a radio show as well. The smaller denomination caused a loss in this perception of him as a community leader, and his exposure was thereafter more limited.

The Sovereignty of God

One area of ministry not closed to him was that of visiting the sick and dying. Santa Cruz was largely a retirement community at that time. Many people were there with no family. He spent a great deal of time visiting the ill, and performed several hundred funerals in less than a decade. It was during these years that he came to see the relevance of the Reformed faith's teaching on the predestination of God.

Too often used as a doctrine of soteriology to be argued, my father came to understand it rather as a doctrine to comfort the saints. Years later, when I asked him about "proof texts" for an ongoing conflict in a Bible study group, he told me not to argue predestination or the sovereignty of God in salvation, as the division was contrary to its intended purpose.

In seminary he had received flack for speaking of predestination, but in speaking with the dying, he realized (with Calvin) it was a doctrine given to comfort and encourage the saints. The dying often wanted to hear that a meaning pervaded death, as well as life, because the alternative was the meaninglessness of both. The sovereignty of God in all things was to him a presupposition, a starting point for our understanding, comfort, and encouragement in Kingdom work.

Early Writings

The pastoral years in Santa Cruz saw the first of my father's book manuscripts. For over a decade, his journals indicate he had been ghost-writing Sunday School lessons for "Douglas"– apparently Earl Leroy Douglas, a PCUSA minister and newspaper columnist who published annual Sunday School lesson material for many years through the Macmillan Company. (The exact nature of his contribution is not stated in his journals.)

In 1958, however, the year he published his first book, *By What Standard?* (on the importance of Cornelius Van Til), that relationship ended, though whether it was because of his departure from the PCUSA or not is unclear.

The next two books reflected his work on education, *Intellectual Schizophrenia* (1961) and *The Messianic Character of American Education* (1963). These two books spurred the creation of a number of Christian day schools in the 1960's and 1970's. Two themes are clear in these books. First, government schools were a statist tool increasingly controlled by a small group of academics intent on using the schools as means of social control by directing its ideologies and values. The public schools were therefore becoming tools of statism by indoctrination from early childhood. The second theme was that Christian parents should desire and pursue a distinctly Christian education for their children as a matter of religious duty.

The second theme appealed to a growing element of the Christian community (cutting across denominational and theological grounds) who were ready to start Christian schools. Often these were husband-wife teams or church-sponsored schools. The first theme, of anti-statism, appealed to the emerging "conservative" movement still trying to find a cohesive and appealing message.

William Volker Fund

My father had desired to spend more time researching and writing for many years. It had been one of his reasons for seeking a rural church upon graduating from seminary in 1944. In the mid-1950's, he began noting his numerous discussions with various individuals and groups on the need for a study center or college of some sort that would represent a counter to the trends toward religious modernism, statism, and socialism.

In 1962 he was hired as a researcher for the William Volker Fund. It was named for a Kansas City, Missouri, businessmen who became a philanthropist. It was entrusted to Volker's nephew Harold W. Luhnow in 1944. He later expanded its charitable work beyond Kansas City, and moved its headquarters to Burlingame, California (just south of San Francisco). Luhnow also began funding conservative and free-market education. Volker money funded the establishment of the Foundation for Economic Education (FEE) in 1946. Its founder, Leonard Reed, coined the term "Libertarian" about that time.

FEE's free teacher seminars educated thousands in free market ideas. Young Americans for Freedom (YAF) was also started with Volker money, as was a student libertarian journal, *The New Individualist Review*, which published articles on abolishing the draft. Richard Nixon picked up the idea, and it became law in 1973.

Luhnow was a proponent of classical liberalism, and he helped subsidize the work of economists F.A. Hayak, Ludwig von Miser, Milton Friedman, and Murray Rothbard. In February 1962, my father was hired by the Fund, and officially began his duties in July.

The Volker Fund was in a state of upheaval at the time. An announcement was made of the Fund's impending dissolution before he began work. It is likely my father felt that any such dissolution would involve the capitalization of spin-off groups with the substantial monies still at its disposal, or that his work would be its last major effort. That appeared to be taking place later that year as the Center for American Studies (CAS) was created as a graduate research center for training, via conferences for clergymen, school teachers, and businessmen. My father was named as "a Christian conservative and a theologian to provide theoretical structure" and to collect the center's library. It sounded like a perfect fit for my father, but it was his theological bent that caused a division at the Center.

Conservative Identity Crisis

The Center soon found itself with an identity crisis. The crux of the issue was the extent of the Christian emphasis of the Center. In early 1963, an early spiral-bound draft of my father's *This Independent Republic* was printed, and about eighty copies mailed out for review. The secular libertarian element saw it as too Christian, too Calvinistic, or too sectarian.

The divide reflected a problem in the developing conservative movement. My father proposed the thesis that America's uniqueness was its heritage of Christian faith, and the outworking of that faith in its culture and institutions, and that a return to that faith and practice was its only hope. But the Volker Fund had spent years investing in secular conservative thinkers as diverse as the atheist Murray Rothbard to the Catholic Intercollegiate Studies Institute and William F. Buckley.

The CAS was intended to focus the Volker fortune on a more specifically Christian message, but the push-back against my father's presuppositionalism and Calvinism surprised Luhnow. Initially supportive and encouraging, he hesitated, then began to pull back. The publication of *This Independent Republic* was postponed. By July, my father had lost the support of Luhnow. He was fired in August of 1963. The next day, he requested a writing grant and it was immediately approved for two years. The emerging conservative movement of the 1960's was unwilling to defend explicitly Christian thinking.

Chalcedon

The writing grant was running out in 1965. A group of conservatives to whom he had spoken asked him to move to Los Angeles and pledged to support his work, if he would start a series of Bible studies and classes. Phil Virtue, a businessman, and Walter Knott, the founder of Knott's Berry Farm– a popular Southern California amusement park– helped pay for his move to Southern California.

It was then he started Chalcedon, which is named after the ecumenical council of A.D. 451. That was already a familiar name in our household, as my father had decided on it sometime earlier. He chose that name for the importance of the council's work and for the central role it played in church history– one few understand.

The Council of Chalcedon ended a centuries-long struggle to defend the doctrine of the incarnation. It is easy for us to take this doctrine for granted. After all, most of the world recognizes the incarnation of Jesus Christ each Christmas as an historical event. It was not so in the early centuries. Prevailing dualistic metaphysical thought equated matter with evil, and said man's real problem was his mortality– that he was flesh and blood. These dualistic views saw matter as the source of evil, and the non-material realm as higher. When the language of Scripture was read by dualists, they interpreted it in this dualistic perspective. Spirituality was understood as a rejection of the material world, a life of asceticism or, at times, self-mutilation and torture. The material realm was seen as evil by nature.

When this false metaphysical view of man looked at Christianity, it tried to fix it, to remove it from the world in order for it to be a truly "spiritual" concept. One of the "fixes" proposed by these dualist gnostics was to deny that Jesus was actually God in human flesh. Such an idea was repugnant to them because of their dualistic view of matter, spirit, and man's problem. The dualists were determined to separate Jesus from human flesh, and they tried many tactics. Every time a council would denounce one tactic as heretical another terminology or explanation would arise.

It was not until A.D. 451 that Chalcedon slammed the door in the face of gnosticism's dualistic denial of the incarnation. Chalcedon declared Jesus was fully God and fully man. In doing so, it declared Jesus Christ to be the only mediator between God and man.

My father saw the implications of Chalcedon as a watershed in history. If Jesus was the one unique, divine mediator, then no person in church or state could claim that role. Both church and state might have ministerial roles, but neither could have sovereign or absolute authority. Chalcedon not only slammed the door on the gnostics, it slammed it on statism and ecclesiastical tyranny. The outworking of the limitation in the west was a progressive denial of power to both church and state and the development of liberty.

The Reformation's rejection of the absolutism of Rome was an application of Chalcedon's definition of Jesus Christ. The English Revolution's denial of the absolute power of the crown and its declaration that it was subject to the law was an application of Chalcedon. The Constitution's limitation of the government to delegated powers was an application of Chalcedon. Liberty is a product of the outworking of Christianity, and the Council of Chalcedon provided the theological basis for what came later, and is not yet fully developed. If Jesus Christ is the only mediator between God and man and He is our Lord, then no claim to sovereignty or rights that belong to Him can be legitimately claimed by any church, state, individual, or institution.

There is more that should be noted about the Council of Chalcedon. Not only did it have long term implications for the future development of the west, the church did not itself welcome many of those implications. Rome rebelled against the implications of Chalcedon regarding human authorities, and moved toward ecclesiastical tyranny. Christian rulers also claimed the right to absolutism as their "divine right." More than defining Jesus Christ, the Council of Chalcedon recognized Who He was and is, and the history of the Kingdom moves in terms of that reality which was confessed– not created– by Chalcedon.

Conservative/Christian

Another movement preceded the formation of Chalcedon. Barry Goldwater, known as "Mr. Conservative," determined to seek the presidency in 1964. Many forget that John F. Kennedy, though personally popular, was not an effective president. He could not get his programs through Congress, and faced strong opposition in his own party. Goldwater, a senator from Arizona, believed he would control the west, south, and mid-west, leaving Kennedy with little more than the electoral votes of New England.

When President Kennedy was assassinated in November, 1963, however, all that changed. Lyndon Baines Johnson, a Texan, was now the incumbent. Constantly invoking the memory of the fallen president, it was Johnson who got the Kennedy programs and more through Congress, and Kennedy was elevated to a cult-like status, his name invoked to further leftist causes for years.

Goldwater's strategy was no longer viable, and he lost in a landslide. Conservatives were shell-shocked, and the Republican party was determined never to allow another grass-roots outsider gain the nomination (they were successful until 2016).

Many of my father's early supporters were Goldwater Republicans. When he went to Southern California nine months after the election, they were discouraged. Many of the concerns posed to him in the following years in the questions and answer sessions of his classes were about the political, cultural, and social revolution underway. People were trying to place things in context. Many of his audience had no previous religious affiliation at all. My father tried to point them to the necessary non-political change that needed to take place, and he came up with a term for it: "Christian Reconstruction."

Like Chalcedon's position in A.D. 451, Christian Reconstruction was a theological understanding, a view that orthodoxy must dictate our faith and action. As with Chalcedon's definition of the incarnation, Christian Reconstruction represented a long-term understanding of the work in the Kingdom. Like Chalcedon's work, it has received push-back from within the church, also largely from those with a dualistic understanding of spirituality.

Theonomy

Chalcedon enabled my father to undertake the study of Biblical Law he had considered in seminary. He began a long series of lectures on the subject which were published in 1973 as *The Institutes of Biblical Law.* This began the modern Theonomy movement.

The antinomianism of the modern evangelical church had been quite apparent for some time, but the effective antinomianism of the Reformed community became readily apparent. Though they rejected the seven dispensations of C.I. Scofield, they effectively held to two dispensation, law and grace, and almost unilaterally rejected Theonomy. My father was often accused of linking the Law to justification, demonstrating such accusers had not so much as read his introduction to the book, which clearly states he was speaking of sanctification and the standard of Christian obedience.

The problem again was dualism in the church. This time, it was not over the nature of our Lord's incarnation, but about the nature of spirituality. Because the Law deals at times with very mundane details of life, it was deemed inferior to what this latest dualism saw as the higher spiritual provision of grace and the leading of the Spirit. Ethics in the twentieth century church had become vague and subjective, so it was no accident that moral problems abounded.

Theonomy is "God's Law," and it is necessary to Christian Reconstruction. We have to build on something certain and secure. We build on God's ethical standard, by His rules. Like Christian Reconstruction, Theonomy is a message that must be embraced; it cannot be imposed. It is a bottom-up understanding of how the Kingdom of God must develop. Its concern about government is primarily the self-government of the believer.

My father's thought was a very comprehensive one, which was inevitable, given his belief in post-millennialism and the inevitable growth of the Kingdom throughout the world until Jesus' enemies are made His footstool, every knee bows, and every tongue confesses His Lordship. My father was merely saying the believer must so bow and confess now, and that such acts are hypocritical without a self-conscious obedience to that Lord and His Law-Word.

The comprehensive, big-picture approach of my father led to a great deal of misapprehension. Many Christian leaders and groups focused on specific moral or social issues, such as education, abortion, or politics. My father spoke of *every* area of thought and action. The secular media saw in his comprehensive theology a political conspiracy to impose a theocracy by force. He was seen as the guiding hand behind individuals and movements who did not have so much as a nebulous contact with him or Christian Reconstruction!

R.J. Rushdoony and Christian Reconstruction became, and still are, a boogey-man in liberal conspiracy thought, though Michael J. McVicar's 2015 book *Christian Reconstruction:*

R.J. Rushdoony and American Religious Conservatism tried to correct that myth. In reality, my father had little use for politics. Christian Reconstruction was about the Kingdom of God, not any state or program. His own political views were closer to libertarian, but he did not at all agree with the man-centered view of authority held by anarchristic libertarians. He believed a biblical order would be very decentralized with no one entity having overall authority.

Protégés

Several brilliant young men began their careers with Chalcedon. My father met Gary North at a student conference in 1962 while working for the Volker Fund. The next year, my father sponsored him as a summer intern there. In 1969, he wrote a piece for the *Chalcedon Report*. In June of 1973, he began a regular column, *An Economic Commentary on the Bible*, which continued until 1981. North's primary focus was, and is, the area of economics. He and my father saw that as an important area for Christian commentary and the introduction of Biblical Law because they both felt that the modern monetary system was based on theft, and would be one of the first areas to suffer a systematic failure. North published *An Introduction to Christian Economics* in 1973, the same year as my father's Institutes.

Greg Bahnsen also began contributing articles to the *Chalcedon Report* on a regular basis in late 1973. Both he and North taught Chalcedon classes in Southern California, though in 1975 Bahnsen was called as a professor of apologetics to Reformed Theological Seminary in Jackson, Mississippi. His time there was tumultuous, primarily after the publication of his *Theonomy in Christian Ethics* in 1977. The faculty was not ready for the seminary to be associated with Theonomy. Bahnsen's area of focus was on apologetics and epistemology from a Van Tillian perspective.

David Chilton also wrote and spoke for Chalcedon during the late 1970's and early 1980's. His focus was eschatology.

In the early 1980's, historian Otto Scott joined the staff of Chalcedon and wrote a regular column. He was also a frequent contributor to "The Easy Chair" tape series. He spoke not only as to political history, but the influence Christianity had on culture.

A History of Ideas

The history of Christian Reconstruction is, thus far, largely a history of ideas and their promulgation. In 1948, Richard M. Weaver's book *Ideas Have Consequences* was published. It is one of the most potent book titles ever, and it has been repeated as proverbial wisdom ever since.

Ideas do have consequences. Bad ideas– like evolution and communism– have done extensive harm and led to millions of deaths, the regression of cultures, and the de-capitalization of Western civilization. Good ideas have a benign effect, and good ideas founded on God's Truth have behind them the certainty of His Word, one that will not return to Him void.

Christian Reconstruction is a theology of the Kingdom of God that points to our responsibility to it. It is a big picture idea. It is not about what we want now or tomorrow so much as our responsibilities now and tomorrow. There is nothing really new about it. It seems like a novelty because the modern church has largely accepted a role of irrelevance, defeat, and weakness.

The power of Christian Reconstruction is in its consistency. The Jewish religious leaders of Christ's day understood His words of resurrection better than the disciples, and the secular world today sees Christian Reconstruction as its antithesis and seeks its repudiation and rejection.

We have been called the "American Taliban," and worse. My father's ideas have often been twisted beyond recognition by those who want to see him vilified. They see a comprehensive worldview that transcends particular political and cultural policy– and they fear it. They are horrified that a theocratic view of history still exists, one that says Christ rules, that He always has, and always will.

The west has retreated from Christianity and liberty, and has returned to statism as a result. But Christianity grows in most of the world. It is the fastest growing religion in the world!

The victory of Christianity will come because the enemies of Jesus Christ are being put down even as He sits at the throne. Christian Reconstruction is not a program that we try to implement, it is an analogy of how we view our responsibility because we believe that victory is certain.

The Core Ideas of Christian Reconstruction

By Mark R. Rushdoony

In 1948, Richard M. Weaver wrote a book with a very profound title: *Ideas Have Consequences*. What we believe to be true shapes our thought and our action. Man is an inherently religious being. He is controlled by his faith– what he believes to be true.

Faith and Ideas

Let me give an example. Enlightenment rationalism was thoroughly humanistic, but was self-conscious about its reliance on God as a "first cause" who put "natural law" into the universe.

That was an idea borrowed from Christianity, but many humanists of the nineteenth century were very unhappy with nominal dependence on God. Darwin tried to sever modern thought from any necessity of dependence on the supernatural, hence the term "naturalism." This is why Darwin was an instant success– there were many who were eager for a new worldview that did not include God. This is why Darwin is the pivotal figure of modern thought.

Darwin's explanation was eagerly received, but it required at least as much faith as the Christian worldview. Even today, the faith continues, though the theory had to change. Darwin believed all changes could be explained by natural selection, by means of what we call genetics. Soon it was obvious that DNA could not produce the huge changes of which Darwin wrote, so an entirely new mechanism was proposed: mutation. So Darwinism was for a time called Neo-Darwinism, in order to reflect this mutation-selection theory. The added element of mutations became the major part of the evolutionary explanation, because Darwin's natural selection theory was not workable.

In 1925, a famous trial took place In Tennessee called the Scopes Trial. The issue of it was the teaching of evolution in public schools. At the time, it was the "Trial of the Century." It was broadcast across the county. For days the defense ridiculed the doctrine of Creationism and a literal interpretation of the Bible. They presented various "scientific proofs" of evolution and called those who did not believe in evolution "ignoramuses." The result was a strong reaction against Creationism.

Churches wanted no part of it and quickly began avoiding the issue by trying to take refuge in the "day-age" or "gap theory" of Genesis. No one was prepared to defend Creationism. What is now often overlooked is that all those proofs that supposedly put evolution on firm scientific ground were eventually found to be either in error or frauds. *None* of them are now used to defend evolution.

The theory has to change. The proofs are found to be contrived, but the theory of naturalism continues. Why? Because the alternative to evolution is a Supreme Being, and modern man's faith will not tolerate such a fundamental paradigm shift.

Ideas do have consequences.

An Alternative Worldview

Evolution is an example of a worldview that that is based on faith. More was at stake than the interpretation of Genesis chapters 1–11, however. Darwinism created a whole new basis by which man was to be understood. He explained origins in terms of chaos and randomness. Man came out of the slime and overcame by force, by violent confrontation, by destroying what interfered with his survival. The "natural law" of Enlightenment rationalism was, by Darwin's thinking, a historical fiction.

This set the pattern for the revolutionary mindset of modern times. Man advances by destroying what is old, dated, and rejected. To retain it is to invite one's demise. Survival requires adapting to change, if not initiating and controlling it.

After the Scopes Trial, Christianity in the west rolled over for a generation, and it still has not recovered. The reasons are varied, but in general, it was because Christianity had ceased to become a world and life view. It had become a purely spiritual exercise that had to do with one's personal life, but not the world. The church gave up Genesis and origins because it was not relevant to personal piety.

There was a reaction to modernism, but it was a retreatist one. The Fundamentalist movement tried to identify the "fundamentals" of the Christian faith and emphasize them, but this came at the price of excluding those somehow deemed less essential to the faith. It was an attempt to hold the line, but was defensive and self-defeating because it only envisioned a church in retreat.

Not too surprisingly, these churches would gravitate to a pessimistic view of the end times, with the belief that things are so bad it means that Jesus is coming back soon. The Fundamentalists shrank in number, while the larger group drifted off into various evangelical branches. Even those that avoided the drift into modernism developed a very pietistic, personalized concept of Christianity.

That was the church in the mid-twentieth century. It was other-worldly in its emphasis. It saw the faith in its personal, but not cultural context. The world was said to belong to the devil. In mid-century, church attendance was still very high and many still identified as Christian, but the culture was spinning away fast.

It was in this context that my father, Rousas John Rushdoony, began his ministry as a pastor in 1944. Since my purpose is to outline the core ideas of Christian Reconstruction, I won't discuss his early ministry. It will suffice to say that the decline in Christianity's impact on the culture was obvious before mid-century. His seminary was liberal. When he went to an Indian reservation in a remote area of Nevada for his first pastorate, he found the Indians considered Christianity to be another cast-off of the white man, something they no longer wanted. My father saw that the problem was with the church, and its limited understanding of the faith and Christian duty.

Christian Reconstruction

In 1965, my father started the Chalcedon Foundation. He began publishing a mimeographed newsletter in October. In his second newsletter, which came to be called the *Chalcedon Report*, he referred to the need to undertake the task of reconstruction. The term dates, then, to 1965, and yet none of the principles of Christian Reconstruction were new. They only seemed new because they challenged the existing evangelical theology that held sway.

Christian Reconstruction is an analogy which describes the responsibility of the Christian to his culture. Christian

Reconstruction says that our culture has problems because it is based on the sinful will of men. Rebellion against God never works, so these problems will progress to a systemic failure. Our current problem is that we're approaching that point in one area after another.

The alternative to accepting further collapse is to rethink and rebuild failing ideas, practices, and institutions– to "reconstruct" based on the Word of God. Christian Reconstruction is not a top-down idea. We start by changing ourselves, and then progress outward to our families, our vocations, and our larger spheres of influence. Christian Reconstruction is a view of the Christian faith and the believer's responsibility to it in terms of the Lordship of Jesus Christ and the reality of His Kingdom.

Christian Reconstruction it is not a centralized organization, so not all reconstructionists agree on all points. My purpose is to address the key points of thinking which gave impetus to Christian Reconstruction and still drive it.

Christian Reconstruction applies Christian responsibility to a worldview. A worldview is nothing more than a big-picture approach to all of life and thought. The Bible certainly gives us a worldview, a "big-picture" understanding of all reality. It begins, after all, with predestination before the foundation of the world, takes us through the creation of time, space, and matter, and ends with a picture of the eternal Kingdom. "Worldview" is a word that merely implies that we have to understand how we fit into this big picture in which we profess to believe.

Christian Reconstruction and the Doctrine of God

Christian Reconstruction begins with a view of the authority of God and His Christ. Genesis records God's creation of all things and His decree to man to exercise dominion over the creation. Then the fall of man is recorded in Genesis 3. Satan's temptation to man was not about a convenient source of food; it was to "be as gods, knowing [or determining as gods] good and evil."

Right away, though, in Genesis 3:15 there was a promise of redemption, and we are told of certain enmity between Satan and the Messiah. That does not mean it was a conflict between equals! In the great commission of Matthew 28:18–20, Jesus declared that He possessed all power in heaven and earth. Then He said, therefore–that is, in light of this authority and power– we, His followers, are to go forth and teach all nations the commands of Jesus Christ.

It is within this context of the absolute authority of Jesus Christ that we preach and teach. We teach a worldview that says, "No man is a god or law unto himself. You cannot determine good and evil on your own authority. All authority belongs to Jesus Christ. Whether you acknowledge it or not, you are answerable to Him."

Christian Reconstruction also assumes a belief in man as fallen, who, if given the latitude, will continually repeat the sin of Genesis 3:5 of trying to assume the rights and prerogatives that belong to God. Because it is theistic, Christian Reconstruction is anti-humanistic, because humanism is nothing more than the elevation of man, as man seeks to remove God from His rightful place.

Christian Reconstruction emphasizes the reality of the fall, but not its legitimacy. It sees sin as real but abnormal, an imposition on God's creation that cannot stand. The believer's calling is to be a new creature in Christ, restored to his created purpose. As Adam was created to work and exercise dominion, so redeemed man– born again in Jesus Christ who Paul called the "last Adam," in I Corinthians 15– is called to exercise dominion in obedient faithfulness.

Christian Reconstruction sees the choice as being man's word and man's law, or God's Word and God's Law. Christian Reconstruction emphasizes God's sovereignty, but not just in Soteriology, the doctrine of salvation. It sees Scripture as fully authoritative because of the sovereign authority of its Author. Because God is God, He can *only* speak with authority.

The Problem of Dualism

We cannot serve two masters. Some things are mutually exclusive. If we love one, we hate the opposite. When Christian reconstructionists propose something, we are immediately confronted with its more popular alternative, and those ideas on which that alternative position is predicated. Sometimes this is perceived as hostile or argumentative, perhaps even unorthodox. Sometimes our antithesis challenges some sacred cows.

One of the sacred cows of the modern church is its view of spirituality, which is dualistic. Dualism is an ancient idea that sees the basic problem of man as metaphysical rather than moral. It predominated in the Hellenic world of the first century. Dualism can share much of the terminology of Scripture without being scriptural. Dualism is a religious idea that sees the spiritual opposed to the material.

Ancient dualism saw matter as inherently evil. Dualism saw man's problem as the fact that he was mortal, flesh and blood. This is why Greek heroes sometimes transcended mortality and became gods (i.e., they joined the higher spiritual realm). This is why the incarnation of God in human flesh was such a contested doctrine in the early church. Dualists did not want to consider that God Himself could be in a mortal body. It did not fit into their dualistic understanding that their pagan thinking brought into the church in the guise of spirituality.

45

Neo-platonism is this specific form of dualism that sees the spiritual as a higher, nobler way. Neo-platonism has always had an influence on the church. It sees spirituality as an "other-worldly" escape from the earthly, mundane aspects of life. It was this dualistic neo-platonism that gave rise to monastic asceticism, and even some notable cases of self-torture and mutilation in the early centuries of the church. What were they thinking? They were thinking in terms of a neo-platonic view of spirituality, which was a pagan view.

It is not too common today for Christians to punish the flesh, but otherworldly spirituality is often presented as superior to earthly mortal concerns. In addition, heaven has, at times, been seen as an ethereal, non-material place where ghostly souls float on clouds.

Dualism in Christian thought has led to pietism; that is, moral ethics based on a subjective view of what is spiritual. "Being spiritual" becomes the goal, instead of obedience. Obedience to commandments is seen as a mundane earthly concern.

Instead of a metaphysical view of reality, Christianity sees it in moral terms. In truth, man's problem is not that he is a mortal, physical being, but that he is a sinner, a rebel against God and His Law. Man, after all, was created a physical being. God called the physical creation "very good." Jesus was in human flesh, yet without sin. Paul told us in I Corinthians 15 that our bodies will be resurrected and then changed, so we will have physical bodies for all eternity. In the Bible, the term "spiritual" is not a reference to the ethereal, but to the things of the Holy Spirit, of the Comforter, who empowers believers in their walk of faith and growth in grace.

I mention Christian Reconstruction's challenge to pietism and a pagan, neo-platonic view of spirituality because it is the nature of reconstruction that some demolition must precede it. We've all seen local efforts to preserve some things in our communities that are headed for redevelopment. There is a debate about what is salvageable and what is not. Some will resist the call for demolition and demand the right to repair unsound structures because they are valued for the personal, family, community, or historic significance.

Likewise, Christian Reconstruction must critique the structures and institutions of our culture. Some of these are old and venerable in the eyes of many, but are rotten, or rest on unsound foundations. Christian Reconstruction, though, is not at heart about demolition but about building anew on a firm foundation. I would like, therefore, to mention some of the positive foundational elements that make up Christian Reconstruction.

Presuppositionalism

Presuppositionalism is an acknowledgement of God's sovereignty, and how we think and understand knowledge itself. It is also about how we use our intellects in relation to the Word of God. Presuppositionalism says we approach God's Word and our own intellect in terms of faith in what God says, rather than our reason. It treats reason as a fallible function of our creaturely, fallen minds. On the other hand, we treat God's Word as truth; we do not test its truthfulness. To question the Word of God is to elevate *our* human reason above *God*, where it sits in judgment on the Creator.

The modern emphasis on the supremacy of reason (rationalism) came from the Enlightenment's revival of Greek humanism. If man is supreme, then man's mind is the ultimate arbiter of true. Greek thought, we should remember, held to a continuity of being. Man was stuck in mortal flesh, but he was of the same nature as the gods, and he could transcend mortality and elevate himself to deity.

Christianity, on the other hand, teaches a Creator–creature distinction, and that man has two limitations. First, man is a creature and he will never transcend creaturehood. Man will always be under the authority of God. Second, man is a sinner and can only be restored to wholeness by grace through the atonement of Jesus Christ.

The late historian Otto Scott once casually expressed to me his dislike of the term "presupposition" because it was redundant. A presupposition is, in fact, a supposition. The term is intentionally redundant. It means that our suppositions, our starting points are themselves based on assumptions. Rationalism says man's mind– his reason– can determine and know truth. Presuppositionalism says man's reason itself is so dependent on his Creator, that knowledge must begin with God's revelation of Himself.

Presuppositionalism is contrasted with all forms of rationalism, particularly evidentialism. The root of evidentialism is "evidence." Evidentialism is the approach of trying to *prove* God exists and that His Word is true. This places man's mind over God and His Word, as man weighs and judges its truth. Faith then becomes mixed with reason. This is why the theological roots of Christian Reconstruction are in the reformed tradition. That tradition sees man's mind as itself fallen, and sees man in need of the regenerating sight given by the Spirit.

Is man's basic problem intellectual, or moral? If you diagnose the disease wrong, you will propose the wrong cure. If man's basic problem is intellectual, he needs more *evidence* to rationally persuade him. The answer to an intellectual problem is to educate men, to encourage a response that teachers see as rational.

If man's basic problem is a moral one, however, his intellect will suppress the truth in unrighteousness (Romans 1: 18). According to the Bible, the origin of man's problem is in the temptation of Eve in Genesis 3: 5. That temptation was not about satiating hunger; it was about the claim that the forbidden fruit would give special powers, namely to "be as gods, knowing good and evil." To "know" good and evil means to *determine* it. Gods do not know good and evil intellectually, they determine it.

It was only after this thought was put in Eve's head that she looked at the fruit and decided it was appealing not just to eat as food, but to make one wise. Man's *intellect* was at the heart of the fall. Presuppositionalism says we must never elevate our mind above that of God. This means reason is always subject to the authority of revelation.

The answer to a moral problem starts with this self-conscious submission to God in repentance and faith. If man's problem is a moral one, he needs more than an intellectual, rational change in his thinking. Man needs a moral change, and this necessitates the grace of God to make him a new creature in Christ. He needs God's grace to believe that God's Word is truth. Salvation by grace received by faith alone is thus the next foundational principle of Christian Reconstruction.

Salvation by Grace Received by Faith Alone

Salvation by grace is the sovereignty of God applied to salvation. Christian Reconstruction has so often challenged the modern church, that it has been accused of being an aberration, even a cult imposed on Christianity. This accusation has taken two common forms.

The non-religious left often accuse us of seeking a top-down, politically imposed agenda. We have been called the "Christian Taliban." This is probably because of our critiques of what is wrong. We do not advocate a slower, conservative humanism. Our critiques serve as a prophetic voice. They are not prophetic in the sense of special revelations about the future, but in the sense of proclaiming the revealed Word of God, of preaching the folly of fighting against the truth of God's moral order. In this sense, we are being prophetic whenever we say, "The wages of sin is death." Christian Reconstruction declares, "As long as we try to be as gods and determine our own good and evil, we will make a mess of our lives and our culture." The message of Christian Reconstruction is so comprehensive, the Left often assumes we can only hope to implement it by a political agenda.

Christian Reconstruction is most often attacked by churchmen with the accusation that we are anti-grace because we believe in God's Law. The tragic assumption of such thinking is that God's Law is in conflict with His grace, and that we must pick one or the other. Such thinking is inherently anti-Trinitarian, because it requires a conflict between the persons of the Trinity. There is no conflict between God's Law and God's grace or between the Father and the Son. Only that which is of the Holy Spirit is truly spiritual, and God's Spirit is never opposed to the law or righteousness of God.

Christian Reconstruction starts with the individual and his regeneration. It is thus entirely within the tradition of the gospel of grace. It is about the out-working of God's regeneration in the life of the believer. Sin cannot be stemmed in our social order until it is stemmed in us. This requires God's grace. Individuals must be born again, be made new men in the last Adam, Jesus Christ. It is important to emphasize that Christian Reconstruction will proceed no faster than the Holy Spirit works. Christian Reconstruction can be proposed, but it cannot be imposed.

Our salvation is totally the work of God's grace in us. Our justification is our declaration of righteousness because Christ's atoning sacrifice is applied to us. The Protestant Reformation represented a split in the Western church over the issue of salvation by grace that is received by faith alone. The Reformers came to a consensus that justification is an act of God's grace received by faith alone.

An issue that was never settled by the Protestant Reformation was sanctification, how we grow in grace, how we learn to serve the Kingdom of God. My father's work on Biblical Law stated in its introduction that it was about sanctification, not justification. It is important to touch on this in discussing the issue of grace, because our sanctification also represents God's grace to us.

All God does for man is of grace. We know the frustration in the expression, "I don't know what you expect of me." God's Law is His revelation to His people of exactly what it is He expects from them. It is also God telling the unbeliever what righteousness/justice looks like. Christian Reconstruction says that God's Law is itself an aspect of His grace to man; it is God telling us what He expects of us.

Think for a moment of the implications of the giving of the Law at Sinai. All the patriarchs had lived in pagan law cultures. More than once Abraham feared his wife would be taken from him by force. Jacob had no legal recourse against the frauds of Laban. Joseph had no recourse against the injustice of being made a slave, or being falsely accused of attempted rape. The friendly relations the Hebrews once had with Egypt turned into outright enslavement. It is not an accident that these injustices are noted in Scripture.

When God freed the Hebrews from slavery, He gave them His righteous Law as a standard by which to live. That was an act of grace. In the introduction to the Law in Exodus 20, God recounted how He had saved them from slavery, and that the culmination of that grace was that they would have His law, true justice. The juxtaposition of slavery and the cruelty of their taskmasters in contrast to their new life under God's Law represented the tremendous shift.

There is a recurring reminder in the prophets that the nation was guilty of multiple instances of injustice because they had progressively abandon God's Law in many areas. The law is thus an aspect of God's grace. We are saved by God's grace and we must live by His grace. Satan's temptation of Genesis 3:5 was a lie. We cannot be as gods. We cannot determine good and evil for ourselves.

Covenant Theology

Another foundational element of Christian Reconstruction is Covenant Theology. This is the sovereignty of God applied to all redemptive history. Covenant Theology holds that God's salvation is one consistent plan throughout Scripture and history, that it is not disjointed by eras or dispensations. Covenant Theology says the history of Abraham and the Jews is part of the Christian church's history.

Dispensationalism is one of those modern ideas that Christian Reconstruction has challenged. Dispensationalism arose in the nineteenth century and became popular in the early twentieth century with the notes C.I. Scofield put in his study Bible. Dispensationalism is the belief that God has dealt differently with people in different periods of history, and that His different plans or dispensations are distinct and only vaguely relevant to our current dispensation, or future ones. Our current unique dispensation is said to be the Church Age. I want to talk about two ways in which Christian Reconstruction challenged dispensationalism. (Dispensationalism involves eschatology– a view of the future– but I first want to address another issue.)

The first way Christian Reconstruction challenged dispensationalism was regarding its view of the past and present. Dispensational theology breaks Scripture into separate parts, each applicable for limited time and a limited audience. According to dispensationalism, the Church Age is entirely distinct from previous and future dispensations. Dispensationalism does not see one plan of redemption and one covenant people throughout Scripture. Dispensationalism's view of the Bible and past redemptive history has had more impact on Christianity than its view of the future.

In 1987, Ross House Books (which is now part of Chalcedon) published a book on Covenant Theology by Charles D. Provan called *The Church Is Israel Now*. That title sums up the heart of Covenant Theology—that the Christian church is heir to the promises and responsibilities of the Hebrew nation of old.

When God called Abraham in Genesis 22:17–18, He promised, "...thy seed shall possess the gates of his enemies." After Peter confessed faith in Jesus Christ as the Messiah, our Lord said "upon this rock (this profession of faith) I will build my church; and the gates of hell shall not prevail against it" (Matthew 16:18). Abraham's seed was promised the gates of his enemies, and then Christ promised that His church would occupy the gates erected by hell itself. Another aspect of that promise to Abraham was that in him "all the nations of the earth" would be blessed. That blessing is Jesus Christ and His salvation. But who is now commanded to teach and baptize "all nations" in the Great Commission? It is the church, the people of Jesus Christ, the heirs of Abraham's faith.

Provan's book lists descriptions of Israel in Scripture. In some cases, he cites where this description is taken away from Israel. Then he gives passages which use these same descriptions as now applied to Christians. Some of these descriptions are specifically stated as belonging to the church: the beloved of God, the children of God, the people of God, the chosen people, and, importantly, "the children of Abraham." What is significant about this book is that it merely lists these passages under outline headings. It is 85 percent Scripture quotes.

It is important to note what the word translated as "church" in the New Testament represents. The New Testament's Greek word for church, ecclesia, is the equivalent of the Old Testament Hebrew word for assembly or congregation, qahal. When William Tyndale first translated the New Testament into English, he used the words "assembly" or "congregation" as the natural translation. Rome was livid, because it liked the organizational, ecclesiastical connotations of the word "church." What his natural translation did was point out the obvious, that the body of new covenant believers is called by the same name as were the old covenant's members.

Some call this covenantal view of the church as the Israel of God "replacement theology," but that is more effective as a pejorative than it is descriptive. In reality, what the book of Acts makes clear is that a great inclusion was taking place as the covenant was expanded to Jew and Gentile alike. The only exclusion referenced by Scripture is the pruning that took place before a grafting in. It is important to note that in horticulture, both pruning and grafting are done prior to periods of growth. The fig tree that bore no fruit (Luke 13:6–9) represented the nation of Israel being rejected as the Kingdom model, because (as Jesus had then been declaring for three years) the new model was the Kingdom of Heaven. Even this represented continuity and expansion, as Jesus was, in fact, heir to David's throne and "King of kings and Lord of lords."

The use of the term "replacement theology" is a little ironic. It is an argument used by dispensationalists, but it accuses Covenant Theology of creating a new dispensation. The difference is they prefer their "Church Age" dispensation to what they characterize as a "replacement of Israel" dispensation. You see, they have to explain what the church is. They explain it as a dispensation not previously revealed. They often refer to it as a parenthesis. In their view, the church has a history distinct from that of Israel, but they believe that nation will once again come to the forefront in the future.

C. I. Scofield believed Christ's death was His backup plan initiated after the people rejected His attempt to establish His earthly Kingdom, and that He will come back again after the Church Age and establish His Kingdom. Dispensationalism told the church that it was in a parenthesis, a holding period, until Christ returns to set up His Kingdom, which was suspended at His death.

Covenant Theology is the view that there's one redemptive history and one covenantal people of God, the church of Jesus Christ. The salvation offered in Genesis 3:15 is found in Jesus Christ, the seed of the woman, and those who believe in Him are the assembly, congregation, or ecclesia of God's people, the church. This is why you have heard the terms "Old Testament saints" or "Old Testament church."

Why is Covenant Theology important? If we are part of the covenant people of God, we have the covenant responsibilities clearly laid out by God. If we are not part of the covenant people of God, then our obligation to God is measured by some other standard that is unique to the Church Age. The most basic question there for the Christian is, "What does God expect of me?"

The Protestant Reformation came to a consensus on justification by grace, but not on sanctification, growth in grace. Different traditions in Protestantism have had different answers for that, and there's still no consensus. Dispensationalism holds that the Old Testament is no longer binding. They believe it is accurate history, and we can mine it for character lessons, but we should not go there for teachings that are binding on the church. Some went so far as to say that gospels are applicable to the future millenniums because the Kingdom was suspended during the Church Age.

Dispensationalism began to unravel when Christians wanted a Biblical way to oppose abortion. They had to go to the Old Testament for texts supporting life in the womb. When evangelicals became involved in politics over moral issues, they again had to turn to the Old Testament.

Dispensationalism has also been wrong about how history would play out since the establishment of the modern state of Israel. The result was that dispensationalism is not nearly as powerful as it was fifty years ago, but its decline has only left a void that no other eschatology has filled.

Postmillennialism

Christian Reconstruction challenged dispensationalism's view of the past and present by means of Covenant Theology. It has also challenged dispensationalism with a different view of the future. Dispensationalism holds that the Kingdom of Heaven of which Jesus spoke has been suspended for 2,000 years, and that it will begin again when He returns and sets up a Jewish kingdom in Jerusalem. That is a very top-down scenario. You can't get any more top-down than expecting God to come and miraculously orchestrate everything! Covenant Theology gives the believer the responsibility to now seek first the Kingdom of

God and His Righteousness. Our Kingdom model has shifted from that of Israel's ancient kingdom to the Kingdom of Heaven, but our responsibilities remain much the same.

Eschatology is not merely academic. Our view of the future dictates what we believe about our present responsibilities. What you believe about your future has a great effect on your thought and actions. You think and act in terms of what you believe is true and certain.

Postmillennialism sees all the references to the Kingdom in the gospels as references to Christ's present rule as King of kings and Lord of lords. The promise of Genesis 3:15 was of a Savior who would crush Satan's head. Postmillennialism believes that happened at Calvary. Jesus said that "the prince of this world is judged" (John 16:11), and that He saw Satan fall from heaven (Luke 10:18). John said Christ's purpose was to destroy the work of the devil (I John 3:8). Paul said Jesus spoiled principalities and powers, and that He made a show of His triumph over them (Colossians 2:15).

The Kingdom of God is now larger and more extensive than it has ever been. There are more Christians in the world today than at any point in history. Postmillennialism sees the Kingdom as now developing towards a maturity that may yet be far into the future. It sees Christ's victory as happening before His return. Psalm 110:1 has the father saying to Jesus Christ, "Sit thou at my right hand, until I make thine enemies thy footstool."

The reference to making another 'a footstool' refers to a common practice of the ancient world. When one king defeated another, the defeated king was brought before the victor where he prostrated himself before the conqueror. The victorious king would put his foot on the head or neck of the conquered king as a visible recognition of his dominion over him. The conqueror could decide to kill him, or to let him rule as a subordinate king, but in either case this was something that took place after the battle was over. Putting the foot on the head of a vanquished foe was a symbolic act done in a court ceremony that came after the battle was over.

The Psalm does not say, "Sit until I send you back so you can fight for your kingdom and defeat your enemies so you will be able to make your enemies your footstool." Moreover, Hebrews 1:3 tells us when Christ sat down on the right hand of the father; it was after he had purged our sins; that is, after His atonement and ascension. So Christ remains at the right hand of the Father until such time as His enemies are defeated and prostrate before Him.

What are the implications of postmillennialism? It means we are engaged in a battle in which a victory is certain. It means we think not as a sub-culture, but as the people of the King, the rightful Ruler of heaven and earth. It means we are authorized to challenge all that is not of God. It means our life and labors have a relevance we cannot see because all things work together for good to them that love God, who are the called according to His purpose.

It means all the parables Jesus spoke of the Kingdom have to do with us and our times, not the future alone. It means we're not in a parenthesis, but in the Kingdom of God and His Christ, and we have work to do as citizens of that Kingdom. It also means that the church of our day is woefully neglectful of its responsibilities if its understanding of Scripture causes it to fail to see its calling.

Biblical Law

Another core tenant of Christian Reconstruction is Biblical Law, or Theonomy. The term "theonomy" comes from two Greek words, theos (God) and nomos (law). It literally means "God's Law." A related word, theocracy, means "the rule of God." Theonomy and theocracy represent the sovereignty of God applied to ethics. In His sovereign rule (theocracy) God has done what all absolute rulers do– He has issued decrees or laws from His throne: theonomy. The extent of the authority of that revealed law constitutes the modern debate about theonomy.

The drift of the modern church into neo-platonic spirituality, together with the dominance of dispensational thought, had caused the church to largely abandon all but the Ten Commandments. My father revived theonomy with his 1973 book *The Institutes of Biblical Law.* When that book was published, dispensationalism completely dominated Protestant eschatological thinking.

Something else also became obvious with the reaction to that book. Many churchmen who never considered themselves dispensational really believed in at least two dispensations, Law and Grace, and they were not about to give up that division. Many reacted to theonomy with great hostility, as if it were a direct assault on the gospel of grace.

This position assumes that grace and law are opposites, and hence incompatible. But grace and law are not opposites. The opposite of law is "lawlessness," which is what theonomy addresses. The opposite of grace (undeserved favor) is getting the punishment for sin we deserve. Just as the opposite of a criminal getting a pardon is no pardon, you could say that the opposite of grace is no grace.

Anti-Statism

Statism is the concentration of power and authority in government. Anti-statism has been a common theme in reconstructionist writings for over fifty years. The reason for this is because man is a sinner. A word that does not appear in the U.S. Constitution but that is now very common is "sovereignty." Sovereignty is an attribute of God—not any man or group of men. Anti-statism can be said to be the doctrine of the sovereignty of God applied to human government.

Humanism is the elevation of man. When the sovereignty of God is denied, it is transferred elsewhere, and thus devolves onto man in some capacity. The elevation of man that humanism represents goes back to the first temptation, to Satan's claim that man can become as god, self-determining and autonomous. When man plays god, the results quickly become ugly.

Humanism thus tends to follow one of two paths. The first is anarchism, the idea that ultimate authority is in the individual. The second is statism, the view that the state is the highest collective voice of mankind, and therefore speaks for the good of all. Anarchy has never lasted very long, but statism has a long and abusive history. Theonomy has a very real governmental concern, but that government with which it is concerned is God's, and the law of His Kingdom.

A society regulated by Biblical Law would have a small, limited government, one that would be protective of liberty. Liberty is essential to the Christian reconstructionist vision. It is not about political solutions. It is not about implementing Biblical Law through a political coup. We have said repeatedly that God's Law cannot be imposed, but must be embraced.

Liberty is important to Christianity because it is the context in which individual self-government, family government, and all other spheres of life thrive. Because government is most often a source of problems rather than their solution, the ultimate political ambitions of Christian Reconstruction, such as they are, are to shrink the power of national and state governments, and to increase liberty.

Dominion

Another fundamental idea of Christian Reconstruction is that of dominion. The dominion of which Christian Reconstruction speaks is not the political dominion of any national or local jurisdiction, but the dominion of God's law in the advance of His Kingdom. It is not the dominion of some man over other men, but the exercise of God's dominion in the earth. It is the exercise of His law over every area of life and thought, in terms of a belief that He is Lord of all. Dominion is man's self-conscious submission to God's Law, theonomy.

Dominion refers to the dominion mandate of Genesis 1: 26–28. Adam was told to exercise dominion, but he chose rebellion instead. Christ, who is called the "last Adam" by Paul (I Corinthians 15:45), calls us to service, and makes us new creatures in Him. Paul tells us to prove what is the good and acceptable and perfect will of God (Romans 12:2). This does not speak of proving the truthfulness or applicability of the Word of God, but of testing what does and does not conform to it. Paul also spoke of the renewing of our minds in that passage. Ideas do have consequences, so we must we think every discipline in terms of the Word of God.

Our philosophy must be based on a theistic footing, not a humanistic one. Economics must be re-thought. Our money is a manipulated, contrived fraud. It constitutes theft by

61

government, and bases our economy on the manipulation of debt, not capital accumulation which is always a product of work and thrift. We must rethink psychology and sociology, beginning not with a mythical evolutionary struggle, but with man's moral problem, his sinful rebellion against God.

We must rethink political science. Liberty will not be restored by the current political system. Modern politics is about controlling the reins of power, but reducing that power. We must rethink our view of diplomacy and the use of military might. Christianity developed the concept of just war, yet it has largely abandoned it.

We must rethink science. Creationism has made great strides, but it needs to go beyond an apologetic of Genesis to be a scientific inquiry based on it. A presuppositional creationism would move science forward, not merely try to prove the Biblical account. We must revive the diaconate and other forms of voluntary charities. We must apply our faith to the arts, to film, TV, literature, and the performing arts.

These areas of dominion are not going to be accomplished through political means, and one of the most important areas in which we need to exercise dominion must never involve the state. We have to start with the church, the ecclesia. Until we have more faithful churchmen, we are still working on the bare foundation of reconstruction. The church needs a more comprehensive theology. It needs an optimistic eschatology. It needs to shed its false dualistic pietism and embrace God's Law-Word as its marching orders. It also needs to tithe. We cannot claim to be doing God's work if we rob Him of what is His.

Christian Reconstruction is not an organization. It is an understanding of the Christian faith, and what God expects of believers. The power of Christian Reconstruction is not in its novelty, for there is nothing really new about it. The power of Christian Reconstruction is in its consistency. That is why secularists often trace every part of the Religious Right to my father and Christian Reconstruction, usually erroneously. The Left sees Christian Reconstruction as a worldview that transcends current political cultural events.

There is power in Christian Reconstruction's assumption that God now rules, that He always has and always will, and that His people and plan are a consistent whole. In terms of this, we walk not by sight but by faith in the fact that Jesus Christ is now victorious, and His victory over men and nations will be revealed in time and history.

An Overview of Theonomy

Mark R Rushdoony

Theonomy is a subject that has evoked very strong reactions in the past generation or so. In 1973, the *Institutes of Biblical Law* by my father R. J. Rushdoony was published by Craig Press, an arm of Presbyterian and Reformed Publishing Company. The reaction of the Reformed community was much the same as that of the Arminian, evangelical community, that God's law was now almost entirely superseded by grace. Many claimed my father was substituting justification by works in place of the Reformation's stand for justification by grace received through faith, proving they had not even read the introduction to the book!

Theonomy comes from two words: theos, meaning "God," and nomos, for "law." Theonomy means "God's Law." It is a descriptive term for the commands God reveals in His Word. That Word further describes man's problem as a moral one: he is a sinner in Adam, whose first sin was disobedience to a specific command of God. Theonomy does not address man's status before God. That is the area of justification. Theonomy is the study of God's Law as the justified man's means of obeying the God to whom he is restored by grace.

Without biblical law, the believer has no definitive standard of obedience. Theonomy says that all men are sinners– even the redeemed. God's Law gives us a foundation for personal righteousness, plus a message to our culture. We can tell it *why* it is failing. Socialism is destructive, for instance, because it is a form of theft. Theft, we can say, is a violation of the law of God and cannot lead to productivity and wealth creation. The law of God works because it reflects the moral certainty of its divine author.

Two Errors Concerning Biblical Law

There have been two errors concerning biblical law that have been a recurring problem in the church. One is an incorrect emphasis on the law, and the other is its negation.

Legalism is the error of believing that the essence of being a real Christian is the technical observance of certain rules. Rather than seeing the law of God as a revelation of God's ethical standard of right and wrong to which regeneration restores us, this error makes God's Law –or man made rules such as the ancient Pharisees'– a tool of man for gaining acceptance by God.

Legalism makes the law of God a rule-book, and compliance a set of technical hurtles man can maneuver. Legalism loses sight of the righteousness of God, and minimizes man's sin nature by focusing on obedience as a minimal required compliance. Legalism often tends to reach a point at which it says, "This is sufficient for God." Legalism makes the law not God's, but man's.

The book of Galatians was written by Paul to counter an early form of legalism that he called "another gospel" (1:6, 8). This was the legalism of the "Judaizers," who wanted to incorporate Christianity within a Pharisaical view of Hebrew religion. They insisted on two things they saw as required of Christians: circumcision, and compulsory adherence to dietary laws. Those were two marks of being a good Jew, and the Judaizers were demanding that converts become Jews in order to be considered Christians. They were making Christianity a subset of Jewish faith, and a Pharisaical one at that.

As a Jew himself, Paul rejected this:

> *"We who are Jews by nature, and not sinners of the*
> *Gentiles, knowing that a man is not justified by the*
> *works of the law, but by the faith of Jesus Christ,*
> *even we have believed in Jesus Christ, that we might*
> *be justified by the faith of Christ, and not by the*
> *works of the law: for by the works of the law shall no*
> *flesh be justified."* (Galatians 2:15-16)

Moreover, Paul revealed something about these false teachers that is very relevant, but often overlooked– their pragmatic motives. *"As many as desire to make a fair show in the flesh, they constrain you to be circumcised; only lest they should suffer persecution for the cross of Christ. For neither they themselves who are circumcised keep the law; but desire to have you circumcised that they made glory in your flesh."* (Galatians 6:12-13)

These verses give Paul's inspired synopsis of the motives of the Judaizers. The Judaizers were not concerned about signs of the covenant (which dietary laws were not). They did not themselves keep the law! They demanded a "fair show in the flesh," an outward compliance.

But why an outward compliance? It was, as Paul stated, because they did not want to "suffer persecution for the cross of Christ." It was necessary to "be Jewish" in order to avoid persecution. Jewish religion was legal in the Roman Empire; Christianity was not. If Christianity maintained that it was a form of Jewish religion, it would remain legal in the Roman Empire. In order to do so, however, certain external conformities to Jewish religious practices were necessary. Before the destruction of Jerusalem in A.D. 70, the Romans considered Christianity a sect of Jewish religion, though Jewish officials tried to suppress it as heretical. After A.D. 70, the old Jewish religious system largely disappeared, and Christianity was a religion without legal status in the empire.

The Judaizers were right in their pragmatic assessment of the legal and political climate, even if they were seeking the cowardly path. It was safer to be a subset of Jewish religion than be separate. There was thus a very real draw to find refuge in the old system, even if it meant pollution by its corrupt legalism. The book of Galatians is not, therefore, directed against the law, but against the legalists who demanded outward Pharisaical conformity.

It must be noted that legalism throughout history often has little or nothing to do with biblical law. Legalism is a demand for outward compliance to any outward standard as the test of true Christianity. These standards have varied widely in different areas and cultures. They have often been dictated by philosophies that have dominated various groups, such as asceticism, dualism, and pietism. The imposition of any requirement that is not required by God is a form of legalism.

In avoiding legalism, however, we must note the other extreme, that of antinomianism. Antinomianism is composed of two words: *anti* meaning "against", and *nomos* meaning "law." It means "anti-law." In theology, it means "against the applicability of God's law."

Antinomianism begins with a perfectly good thesis: "We are saved by the grace of God which we received by faith alone; we are not saved by the law." Then, however, antinomianism draws an unwarranted inference: "Grace has replaced the law and the two are antithetical. We cannot have both law and grace." This supposition must be challenged.

Law and grace are not opposites. Grace is the unmerited favor of God. Grace can be any such favor, but we usually speak of it in terms of the redemption of man and his justification through faith in the sacrifice of Jesus for our sin. In that light, the opposite of God's grace is the absence of it, His wrath and judgment. The opposite of law is lawlessness (antinomianism). What Scripture contrasts to grace is not law, but works. The New Testament describes a misuse of the law. However, it is not its use as a standard of obedience– sanctification– but its use as a means of justification.

> "Christ is become of no effect on you, whosoever of you are justified by the law; ye are fallen from grace." (Galatians 5:4)

The Nature of God and the Law

It is dangerous to juxtapose two things which both stem from God's nature– His justice (law) and His grace. It is, after all, the law of God and the grace of God we are considering. Ought we not approach the law of God and the grace of God as harmoniously reflecting the one God Whose attributes include justness as well as love and mercy? Moreover, if the just law of God which required death for sin was submitted to by God incarnate in Jesus Christ, dare we consider that law in conflict with His grace in assuming it?

Did not Jesus' act of submission to the law ratify its just, binding nature? Jesus repeatedly defied the false religious rules of the religious leaders of His day. By submitting Himself to death in terms of God's Law (Genesis 2:17), He was declaring its validity with His act of grace. Moreover, we profess both faith and repentance in conversion as our faith in Christ's work acknowledges our sin and liability for the penalty of the law, if it were not for His grace.

The early church spent four centuries battling over the correct understanding of the godhead. The fight was not an academic one, but represented the long conflict with dualism's attempt to define away the incarnation of God in human flesh. Most religions held to a dualistic (sometimes tripartite) view of man, a view of reality that saw matter as inherently evil, and the physical world as evil. Religion to dualism was an escape from the material realm. This view supposed man had a metaphysical problem (he was a material being) rather than a moral one (that he was a sinner.) As a result, dualists tried to draw Christianity back in to these pagan philosophical divisions.

Many in the early church fought such tendencies. For many years, the conflict focused on the nature of the incarnation. The dualists felt they were protecting God from being polluted by association with matter by denying that Jesus was truly incarnate. They tried in various ways over the centuries, but a succession of church councils and creeds closed the door on each new attempt to circumvent the doctrine of the incarnation. In defending the nature of the incarnate Jesus, the early church fathers fought to defend the doctrine of the Trinity for four centuries, until they finally won with the Council of Chalcedon in A.D. 451.

Generations of church fathers rightly saw the equality of the persons of the Trinity as essential. The doctrine of the Trinity is now under greater attack than ever before. Much of this attack has come from the attacks on Biblical law, because antinomianism has often created arbitrary and distinct attributes amongst the three persons. The Father is said to be the God of law, justice and wrath. Jesus is said to be the God of love and mercy. The Spirit is said to be our enabler and empowerer. None of these are incorrect until they limit these attributes to one person of the Trinity, or put their administration by one person of the Trinity in conflict with the nature or works of another.

Such a view is not merely an unorthodox understanding; it introduces tension and even a systemic schizophrenia into the godhead to such an extent men feel compelled to choose between them. Some Christian groups emphasize either Jesus or the Holy Spirit. The "law versus grace" scenario pits God the Father against God the Son. A

Trinitarian faith will hold the work of the Father, Son, and Holy Spirit to be one. As the Quicumque vult –also known as the Athanasian Creed– made clear here in part:

> "Whosoever will be saved, before all things it is necessary that he hold the catholic faith; Which faith, except every one do keep whole and undefiled, without doubt he shall perish everlastingly.

In the catholic faith this is:

> That we worship one God in Trinity, and Trinity in Unity; Neither confounding the persons nor dividing the substance.
>
> For there is one person of the Father, another of the Son, and another of the Holy Spirit.
>
> But the Godhead of the Father, of the Son, and of the Holy Spirit is all one, the glory equal, the majesty coeternal.
>
> Such as the Father is, such is the Son, and such is the Holy Spirit...
>
> So likewise the Father is Lord, the Son Lord, and the Holy Spirit Lord; and yet they are not three Lords but one Lord...
>
> And in this Trinity none is afore or after another; none is a greater or less than another, But the whole three persons are coeternal, and coequal. So that in all things, as aforesaid, the Unity in Trinity and the Trinity in Unity is to be worshipped.
>
> He therefore that will be saved must thus think of the Trinity."

Martin Luther called the Athanasian Creed the greatest statement of the church to his day, and for good reason. We would do well to remember its rigorous commitment to the "Trinity in Unity." Though the works and manifestations of the three persons of the Trinity are at times clearly distinct, they are in perfect unity of purpose. To suppose a "conflict of interest" in the godhead by opposing the persons or their work is to introduce an ancient pagan idea of deity. Man's conflict comes from his rebellion against the perfect harmony of the godhead. It is sinful man that is conflicted, not God, and man's thinking often reflects this struggle.

Seeing the harmony of the Law of God and the grace of God should only be one aspect of our understanding of "God in Trinity, and Trinity in Unity." Academic categorizing of the Word of God may be useful in understanding it, but is misused as a means of limiting that Word.

Distinguishing a law as "civil" in its application should not be used to imply it is not a moral law, for ultimately every word of God is a moral certainty, because God only speaks absolute truth. The law in its entirety is thus, as Pierre Courthial notes, often referred to in Scripture using the same attributes as the Law-Giver, the Triune God:

The Lord is Spirit (John 4:24); the law likewise is spiritual (Romans 7:14). The Lord is Holy – He is qualitatively distinct from His creation (Psalm 22:3; Isaiah 6:3; Revelation 4:8); He is the Righteous One, the Just One (Psalm 7:10; Acts 3:14); He is Good (Psalm 145:9; Matthew 19:17). His Law, as a reflection of Who He is, is likewise "holy, just, and good" (Romans 7:12; cf. Psalm 119).

Theonomy and Covenant

There is also unity in the Triune God's dealings with man. "For I am the Lord, I change not," God says of Himself

(Malachi 3:6). Theonomy is more than a belief in God's Law as a topic of study; all concede there are laws in Scripture. Theonomy is a belief in something about God's Law, namely, that it is a perpetual revelation of God's unchanging ethical standard. Those ethical standards are seen not as temporary rules, but as revelatory of the nature of God and His will (law) for those He draws to Himself in covenant.

The covenanting God is the same God Who changes not, so theonomy naturally flows from a theology (study or understanding of God) that sees unity in His dealings with men. As opposed to dispensationalism– the influence of which peaked in the west in the mid twentieth century– covenant theology sees a continuity in God's dealings with men, rather than a discontinuity. One covenant of grace is thus in view from Eden to the eternal Kingdom.

Pierre Courthial refers to his overview of redemptive history as a "covenantal synthesis," with successive "covenants" as "successive manifestations" of the single unfolding "Covenant of Grace." The word covenant first appears in Genesis regarding Noah, but the covenant of grace had existed at least as early as Genesis 3:15, where Satan was addressed, "And I will put enmity between thee and the woman, and between thy seed and her seed; it shall bruise thy head, and thou shalt bruise his heel."

When God "established" His covenant with Noah, He was ratifying or confirming His covenant of Genesis 3:15 to maintain a seed of the woman that would crush the head of the serpent. The godly line from Adam to Noah was the Sethites.

When we speak of grace, we tend to focus on the saving grace of God to man after the fall; yet, all things God gives His creatures are of grace as well. God's prerogative to command is often referenced in Scripture in the context of His right as Creator, an allusion which places man, as a creature, in a position of dependence on divine provision. A covenant of grace thus existed in Eden before the fall.

The dominion mandate (Genesis 1:28) was an unmerited blessing on man. Genesis 2 tells us that God placed a tree of life in Eden (v.9) before He placed a man there (v.15). The grace of God was evident in the creation of Adam, the divine benediction on man prior to the dominion mandate, and by the provision of the tree of life. Grace is thus clearly revealed prior to law (the forbidden tree, vs. 16-17), leading Courthial to refer to these blessings and commands as "Gospel and Law," with the very sight of the forbidden tree of the knowledge of good and evil a constant reminder of their place under God's Law.

Even before sin, there was this theonomic context to Eden. The sin of Adam and Eve was rebellion against that law in favor of one of their own choosing: their desire to make good Satan's phony promise that they could "be as gods, knowing good and evil" (Genesis 3:5). Gods do not know good and evil rationally, they *determine* them, and it was this desire for autonomy (autos, "self," and nomos, "law," or "self [made] law") as opposed to theonomy (God's law) that was the heart of the first sin.

Abraham's Seed

The covenant of grace that began in the promise of Genesis 3:15 continued through the line of Seth to Noah and his sons. It involved a genetic line of descent that became progressively more defined with the calling of Abraham and then Jacob, Judah, and the royal line of David. The covenant with the descendants of Abraham furthered the three great covenantal promises made to him, that a people would originate from him and that they would be a holy people, a land would be theirs, and that a universal blessing would result.

In order to understand the covenant to Abraham, we must understand it in terms of the original covenant promise of the seed of the woman who would crush the head of Satan. The promises to Abraham and all God's gracious dealings with Israel were directed towards the fulfillment of that promise, the Messiah. As men tend to do with God's gifts, the Jews by the time of our Lord had become so focused on God's grace to them that they had come to see it as theirs by right.

The purpose of the promises to Abraham was the coming of the Messiah, incarnate God in the person of Jesus of Nazareth. The genealogies showed his descent from the promised line specifically through David. Salvation was "of the Jews" (John 4:22) not as a racial or ethnic necessity, but as a covenantal necessity. It is no accident that all such genealogical records, and even tribal distinctions, were lost a generation after the crucifixion of our Lord with the destruction of Jerusalem. They were no longer necessary to redemptive history, as their crucial information was preserved in Scripture, their accuracy attested by the fact that there is no record of any objection to the genealogies when the records were readily available before A.D. 70. Likewise, the land protected the nation and the promised line. Jesus Christ was Himself the universal blessing.

A theology that sees a single covenant progressively developed and revealed (which not even the disciples fully understood until after the resurrection) has implications beyond theonomy. Not only does one unchanging God imply "one covenant" and "one covenant law," it implies one covenant people. The Greek term for "church" in the New Testament is "ecclesia," the congregation or assembly, and is the Greek equivalent of the Old Testament word, so translated. The body of Christ, the ecclesia or "church," is referred to by the same language as the congregation of Israel, an identity that would be presumptuous if it were not by divine inspiration. The implications are clear: the body of Jesus Christ, the church/ecclesia is the true Israel.

To call this "replacement" ignores the continuity that is in clear view. The twelve disciples became the new patriarchs of what was at first a very Jewish ecclesia. In the words of Paul, there was some pruning of dead wood, and new branches were grafted in. But the illustration of grafting implies a continuous life in the vine, as it was only in the Messiah that either Jew or Gentile had salvation. The ecclesia is the true Israel, not the new or alternate Israel.

The three promises to Abraham were clearly applicable to the Jews, but have in Christ now been enlarged and expanded. The old Kingdom of Israel model has been expanded to the larger Kingdom of Heaven, where Christ reigns as King of kings and Lord of lords. That gospel of the "Kingdom of Heaven" was the gospel preached by John, and then by our Lord (Matt. 3:2; Mark 1:14). The three promises to Abraham were focused on a limited place and people, up to the advent of that kingdom. After that, the promises were expanded to "all nations." The people promised to Abraham was enlarged and expanded, not replaced. The land now extends to use the far isles, and Zion is now wherever the kingdom of God is established, as the universal blessing, in which all could find the grace of God which extends wherever the Holy Spirit sends His regenerating power.

In this understanding of the covenant, Christianity is seen not as a new religion but as the faith of Abraham. That patriarch longed to see the day of Jesus Christ, and, our Lord said, he did so (John 8:56). By faith he believed the day was coming, saw its certainty, and "was glad." The corrupt priesthood which orchestrated the death of the Messiah it professed was destroyed in A.D. 70. All records of Levitical, Aaronic descent were lost, and the hereditary lines hopelessly mingled so that the old system can never be revived. What we call "orthodox Judaism" is not the faith of Abraham, but a system developed after A.D. 70 to keep some semblance of unity amongst the scattered, unbelieving Jews. It was based on rabbinical traditions, and is best understood as an institutionalized form of Pharisaism.

What does this understanding of the covenant have to do with theonomy, then? If we, as the assembly or congregation of Israel, are part of the renewed covenant ("New Testament in my blood") that was promised to Adam and defined to Abraham, then we must see the "one law" that governs the "one covenant." Even those aspects of the law fulfilled in Jesus are still valid in His Fulfillment. Christians must claim the binding requirement of blood sacrifice, for instance, even though we do not practice it. The blood sacrifice of Jesus Christ, the Lamb of God, is our once and final blood sacrifice, but its legitimacy and permanence remain, as the slain Lamb even now sits by the throne of God.

Moses and Grace

All God's dealings with man are of grace. Only man was created in the image of God, which His Word associates with knowledge (Col. 3:10), righteousness, and holiness (Eph. 4:24). He was created to exercise authority over the creation (Gen. 1:26). God's blessing on man was a benediction, a pronouncement of blessedness on man which was then followed by his commission, the dominion mandate (v. 28). Eden was a place that excelled as an environment for man's work. The tree of life was at its center, a constant reminder of God's gracious provision. God's grace proceeded and was the context for His law in Eden, the tree of the knowledge of good and evil (Gen. 2:8-9, 16-17).

When Adam and Eve fell, God first pronounced a promise of Satan's defeat that would come though the seed of the woman (Gen. 3:15). Only after that act of grace did He pronounce punishment on Eve (v.16) and Adam (v.17-20). Adam saw the grace in God's promise, as his name for his wife was Eve– "life-giver"– an optimistic reference, given his previous attempt to shift the blame to her. We then see in the verses that follow, worship in the form of sacrifices.

Adam and Even were, throughout their lives (930 years in Adam's case), probably more keenly aware of God's grace than any modern evangelical. Ours is an awareness of understanding enabled by the Holy Spirit. Adam and Eve had a unique understanding based on experience. In their pre-fall state, they knew the grace of God as well as His law, and the certainty of death. When they sinned, they hid from God because they were guilty of a capital offense (naked before God in every sense). Anything less than death was a gracious gift of God's longsuffering.

For nine hundred thirty years (and Eve, an unknown lifespan) Adam experienced the grace of God. When her first child was born, Eve saw him as "a man from God." Her thinking was of God's grace and in the context of the promised "seed of the woman." Adam and Eve knew, without any self-delusion, that their punishment was part of the righteous nature of God, and yet they rested in a future directed by His gracious hope.

The law was itself a gift of grace. Genesis briefly surveys the dangers and uncertainties of the patriarchal period. Lot was kidnapped by a neighboring warlord. Abraham had to fund a private militia to free him. We are told of the total degeneracy of Sodom and Gomorrah. Twice, Abraham felt it was likely a king would kill him and force Sarah into his harem (to then control all of her family wealth), and saw no way to escape.

Later, Jacob was cheated by Laban, but had no legal recourse. Laban was likely the patriarchal "law" of the area (he also stole the dowries of his daughters, Rachel and Leah). Jacob's only recourse was to flee further injustice. Joseph was sold as a slave, yet had absolutely no legal recourse. Later he was imprisoned for rape, an accusation from which he was never vindicated; he was only freed because he was deemed useful to the pharaoh. The family of Joseph then migrated to Egypt on friendly, even welcoming terms, only later to be turned into slave laborers. When the political rulers of Egypt wanted to curb the growth of the Hebrew population, it ordered the execution of children. A common thread in these historical vignettes is the injustice that prevailed, and the vulnerability of the line of promise whose patriarchs had no recourse to justice. The powerful ruled at will. The law was what the tyrant said it was. It was into this brutal context that God gave His Law.

The Law of God given through Moses was itself a gift of grace because it was, unlike the law of all surrounding peoples, God's. It was perfect justice because it was a revelation of the attributes of God. As we read Scripture, we should note that justice is a moral fact, not an abstract fact that judges value. There is, in fact, no distinction between the words justice and righteousness in Scripture; the two words are but different English words for a single word in the Hebrew as well as in the Greek. We see this common meaning in references to those justified by grace through faith. They are referred to alternately as "the just" or "the righteous," and justification is often properly defined as a "declaration of righteousness."

The opportunity after Sinai to live under laws that God declared to be righteous/just was its own blessing: "Ye shall therefore keep my statutes, and my judgments: which if a man do, he shall live in them: I am the Lord." (Lev. 18:5)

This was a passage later quoted by Ezekiel when describing the consequences of their disregard for the law (Ez. 20:11, 21). Years later, Nehemiah describes the Levites, new again in the land, publicly proclaiming faithfulness. This Leviticus 18:5 passage was then again quoted by the Levites as revealing the foolishness of rebelling against the statutes of God "which if a man do, he shall live in them" (Neh. 9:29). The life implied here refers to more than the absence of death by God's judgment. The word translated as "live" in Leviticus 18:5 and Nehemiah 9:29 is variously translated as "quicken, revive, recover, preserve, nourish, or repair." The meaning of "live" is opposed to the rebellion and failure to obey which resulted in oppression, subservience to others, and being given over to "the hand of their enemies" (v.28). Living under God's Law was more than a command; it was its own blessing, a grace from God which allowed them to "live" life under God's justice and His beatitude rather than His judgment.

The corresponding negative declaration to living in God's Law, more common in the prophets, was that the injustices in Israel were themselves cause for judgment, because they would not exist if the laws of God were being followed. Time and again, the prophets pointed to injustices that prevailed as the evidence of violating the law. Amos pointed to the theft of wage from the poor (5:11) and rigged scales and debased currency (8:5) as forms of theft. In preference to the formalities of worship and ritual, even sacrifices, the prophet said God wanted to see "judgment run down as waters, and righteousness as a mighty stream" (5:20-24). Abuse of workers was apparently common when God's Law was not followed (Micah 3:3, 9, 10). The property of the poor was being transferred to the oppressors (Is. 3:14) and their lands acquired (5:8).

All this was characterized not just as unforeseen consequences of disobedience, but as a rejection of justice (29:20-21). Not just an omission was involved; failure to abide by God's laws represented a refusal to implement true justice. James repeated the same condemnation of injustice by the rich. The power their wealth gave them was used to defraud workers (James 5:4-6). For that reason alone, miseries would come to them (v.1) when the Lord came in judgment (v.8).

The law of God as a whole is a gift of grace, but the specific laws are gracious as well, because man needs specific moral direction. Just as Adam and Eve were, before sin, given very specific moral rules in Eden regarding the tree of the knowledge of good and evil, so redeemed man also needs specificity in ethics. The fact that we do not understand the reason for those ethical lines in irrelevant. In sinlessness Adam and Eve did not understand the reason for the prohibition on the forbidden tree, and in our regeneration, we do not always understand the reason for the lines established by God's Law.

Adam and Eve sinned because they believed Satan's lies, and thought they knew why God had given them that prohibition. They made the rational decision that disobedience would lead to a higher spiritual plane "as gods." That rationalism led to the fall. Likewise, antinomianism believes that abandoning the specifics of God's Law leads us more into a greater grace and spirituality.

Rather, everything in the garden was a gift of grace, including the one single law from the mouth of the Creator. To the Hebrews at Sinai, God's Law was a breath of fresh air, a life in terms of true justice, a grace to both live by and one in which they truly lived a fuller life.

The Relationship of Man to the Law

Man in rebellion against God is at "enmity" with God, "not subject to the Law of God" so he "cannot please God" (Rom. 8:7-8). The Law of God in its entirety, including the law of Genesis 2 and the curse of Gen. 3, represented a criminal indictment, a "handwriting of ordinances" against the sinner.

The conversion of the indicted sinner involves repentance and faith. On conviction by the regenerating Spirit, a man sees his state before God and, in repentance, seeks mercy. Faith is a reliance on the substitutionary atonement of Jesus Christ as satisfying one's own death penalty. This death penalty for sin that we acknowledge was necessitated by the righteous standard of God's Law. The regenerated man is said to be justified, which means "declared righteous" by God. We can think of this as coming condemned before God's court. Rather than treating us as condemned men, God as Judge recognizes our sentence as paid in full by Jesus. This justification is an act of God, not a process or a work of man. This is what Paul referred to when he said, "Therefore we conclude that a man is justified by faith without the deeds of the law" (Rom. 3:28).

Saved from the curse, we are called to a new life under "the law of the Spirit of life in Christ" (Rom. 8:2) as a "new creature" in him (II Cor. 5:17). At the end of Romans 3, just after describing justification by faith as excluding works, Paul asked and then answered a question. "Do we then make void the law through faith? God forbid: yea, we establish the law" (Rom. 3:31). Paul was very clear that justification was not by "the deeds of the law" but did, in fact, establish the law. How can that be?

Paul was excluding the law as a means of man's justification because that is an act of God. He did not exclude the law as a means of obedience and man's sanctification.

Sanctification is the justified, righteous man's growth in grace, his maturation in terms of the regenerating power of the Holy Spirit, his increasing ability to reject sin and obey God. As such, sanctification is an ongoing process in the life of the believer. The only objective standard for obedience given by God is His law-word.

The law of God is sometimes presented in Scripture as a negative, a threat to man. But to whom is it a threat? The man on death row is there because of the sentence of the law. To him, the law is his curse. The redeemed man has had his death penalty paid. The law is no longer his curse; it now represents his liberty, because it represents his new life. To the pardoned man, the law represents his protection as well. If a pardoned man repudiated the law altogether, he would be rejecting his need for pardon and, in fact, advocating the rebellion for which he was pardoned. Antinomianism in the church represents those who claim the pardon of God, still embracing rebellion against His law as their right.

The same Paul who wrote that through faith "we establish the law" (Rom. 3:31) also wrote the words which caused Luther to slam the door on works-based righteousness: "The just shall live by faith" (1:17). The Reformation that resulted from Luther's epiphany was principally centered on justification by grace received by faith alone. I believe this is a correct understanding, but it was not Paul's primary point in Romans 1:17. He was not talking about his conversion at all, but something far more recent in his life. Paul was speaking of his desire to see those in Rome, but was emphasizing his need to preach to "other Gentiles," to "Greeks, and to the Barbarians" (v.13-14). It was his drive to preach the gospel that precipitated his statement, that "the just shall live by faith." The reason he says that is because it was through the preaching of the gospel that "the righteousness of God [is] revealed from faith to faith."

The "righteousness" of God is His justice, which clearly involves the sinner's need for justification, but Paul was talking about the necessity of preaching and surrendering his preference to visit Rome because of his more urgent mandate to preach the gospel. It was in terms of this necessity that Paul reminded the Romans that "the just shall live by faith." He notes it as a quotation from Scripture. That text is Habakkuk 2:4 which reads, significantly, "the just shall live by his faith," adding the word "his." The context of the prophet's words is also important. It was said in speaking of the necessity of standing in terms of the certainty of God's prophetic word that Habakkuk said, "The just shall live by his faith." The emphasis is clearly on the word "by." The just/righteous man lives in terms of his faith.

Both Habakkuk and Paul referenced their duty to act in terms of their faith. That is a reference to sanctification, submitting ourselves and our day-to-day living to God. Faith is the means we receive justification, and it is in terms of our faith that we live and act as new creatures in Christ. We live by/in terms of our faith.

Man's problem is sin. The fall produced two great problems for man, neither of which he could solve. The first was restoration to fellowship with God. The fall was immediately followed by God's promise (covenant) of the defeat of Satan. The Old Testament traces the development of God's restoration of man which culminated in the atonement and resurrection. The second great problem was that of ethics and morality (applied ethics). It was the desire to be "as gods knowing good and evil" (Gen. 3:5) that was the root of the first sin. Adam and Eve first decided they could determine good and evil for themselves. It was only after this idea took root in them that the fruit seemed desirable (3:6). The first sin was a presumptuous determination of man that God's law was superseded.

The gospels represent the incarnation and inauguration of the last days, the Kingdom of God. The apostolic writings which followed describe the advance of that kingdom and instruction for believers. The entire Bible is about man's recall to newness of life in Jesus Christ.

The Westminster Shorter Catechism's first question asks, "What is the chief end of man?" The answer is "Man's chief end is to glorify God and to enjoy him forever." Modern Christianity has often made the faith man-centered by focusing on eternal salvation and the blessings God gives man, while neglecting man's call to serve God. Glorifying God requires sanctification and its resultant obedience. We do not accidentally, incidentally, or coincidentally obey God.

Theonomy is the theology that says man's ethical standard is in God, and our moral standard, our specific application of God's ethics to life, is in His law. The implications are far-reaching. Man cannot glorify God while violating His commands. Theonomy is not a social goal, but an understanding of a reality that binds man to God's ethical standards; all men are now, as always, under "God's law." The modern theonomy movement is an effort to make the church of Jesus Christ self-conscious of that current reality so that it responds with a desire to obey God.

Antinomianism in the Church

Antinomianism has been a recurring problem in the church. This was an issue which was not settled in the Protestant Reformation, which dealt principally with the doctrine of justification by grace received through faith. That position was established in Protestantism, but the means of sanctification, growth in grace, was not. No consensus on the means of sanctification was reached by the reformers, though in practice, pietism has been a prominent, recurring idea in the church, particularly since the Enlightenment.

Because of the emphasis on justification, both Luther and Calvin can appear quite antinomian. One has to take into consideration whether their negative comments on the law are in reference to the matter of justification or not. When they referred to ethics, the law was often spoken of in a favorable light, though due to their lack of focus on sanctification, their thinking was not always consistent. In 1527 Luther wrote that pastors should teach and enforce the Ten Commandments.

John Agricola wrote this was a compromise on the doctrine of justification, demonstrating that the confusion of that doctrine and sanctification is not a new one. Agricola wrote, "Art thou steeped in sin – an adulterer or a thief? If thou believest, thou art in salvation. All who follow Moses must go to the Devil; to the gallows with Moses." Such logic still prevails in Protestantism. It says the law of Moses was a different salvation that is now so anti-grace that it is evil, and that salvation by faith requires the believer to renounce the law as carnal. The modern equivalent of Agricola's idea is the lawless evangelical Christian, who's only "standard" of obedience is a vague leading of the Holy Spirit. Too few such evangelicals stop to question whether the subjective leading of God's Spirit would ever conflict with the Word of the Triune God: Father, Son, and Spirit ("God in Trinity, and Trinity in Unity".)

When the law is wrongly seen as in conflict with grace, then it naturally becomes abhorrent, yet the law of God was never a way of salvation. It is only anti-Christ when it is falsely used legalistically, as a means of salvation, as Paul makes clear in Galatians. The law is not the enemy of the redeemed, but of the unredeemed, because it represents his death sentence.

Antinomianism proposes a lawless Christianity, which is an oxymoron. The moral law of God was so serious that one breech necessitated the death penalty, so serious no sinful man could pay its penalty, so serious only incarnate God could pay its penalty. Antinomianism proposes that God required the death penalty, then abandoned it altogether in favor of a subjective spiritual standard.

Theonomy posits that Christ's atonement was not the abandonment of God's Law, but the payment of its penalty. Our faith must be in both Christ's atonement and the justness of God's Law that condemns us and necessitated His sacrifice.

A popular hymn sung in many Protestant churches in my youth was "Trust and Obey." Those churches were in general agreement on what was meant by trust, or faith. That was the legacy of the Reformation. There has never been a consensus on how obedience is to be measured, on sanctification. This is, Theonomists hold, the next needed reformation in the church.

Theonomists often do sound like negative, complaining voices in the church, for they are the modern "protestors" against contemporary Christianity's lack of ethical mooring.

The Implications of Antinomianism

Theonomy and Antinomianism are theological, not philosophical, positions. The issue is God's Law or not God's Law; it is not a debate of God's Law or no law. Antinomians will posit a law. If it is not God's Law they posit, it will be another. All such "law" deemed acceptable to man is thus of human origin, or at least selection.

God's objective standard is replaced in antinomianism with a subjective standard. Because that standard (which, being subjective is, in reality, many standards) is subjective, it will never be met with the scrutiny of theonomy, which claims the authority of "Thus saith the Lord..."

The lawlessness of a culture cannot be addressed by an antinomian church. The church then loses its voice because it cannot address issues with specificity. Why turn to God's Law when the church has abandoned it? If a civil law is deemed archaic, courts will not allow its prosecution. District attorneys will no longer make the effort to do so, and police will stop citing offenders. The message is that the law can be ignored with impunity, and citizens will act as if the law is irrelevant, even if it is technically still on the books. Likewise, when churches deem God's Law as no longer binding, they stop teaching its authority or warning men against its violation. The message of the church is that God's Law can be ignored, so its moral authority is effectively renounced.

There have been many forms of subjective morality in the church. A recent form (actually a revival of a nineteenth century idea) was "What Would Jesus Do?" This approach neglected the Word of the Triune God revealed in Scripture and replaced obedience with good intentions. "Love," "brotherhood," and "toleration" have also been used as universal principles to govern our behavior, all of which are abstract concepts that replace specific obligation. Another common subjective "standard" (though really, again, the absence of one) is "the leading of the Spirit."

Categorizing God's Law can be helpful, but we must be careful not to create false distinctions by categories that are then used to dismiss some or all of the law. A well-known distinction is to divide the laws into "moral," "civil," and "ceremonial" categories. The Ten Commandments are often said to be the moral law and therefore all that is binding on the Christian. To reduce only those to the status of "moral" is arbitrary. It suggests the other commands have no moral authority.

The ceremonial law is almost universally said to be no longer binding. That is a half-truth. Hebrews makes clear that Christ fulfilled the functions of priest and sacrifice, meaning the temple observances are no longer needed because the reality in Him has replaced the type, or shadow of His work now accomplished.

Still, we believe in blood sacrifice. We do not practice it because Christ is the Lamb of God that taketh away the sin of the world, but we still believe in it. We do not practice priesthood or the rituals of the temple because Christ is our High Priest, but we still believe in it. Even the ceremonial laws are perpetually valid in Jesus Christ.

A third category that is even less helpful is that of "Hebraic civil laws." The categorical name is often used to imply "for Hebrews then but for no others." Yet the civil laws were specific applications of the moral law. The older term for this was casuistry. Though often used in a negative sense, now it refers to the application of moral principles to new instances. A more modern legal term which my father used in *The Institutes of Biblical Law (1973)* is "case law."

Paul used case law regarding theft in I Corinthians 9:1-14 and I Timothy 5:17-18. This follows Scripture's reference to the statutes or "commandments" on the one hand and "judgments" or "testimonies" on the other. The commandments are the principles which override the Ten Commandments, and the judgments or testimonies are their applications, the "case" (or case-by-case) law. The specific laws cannot then be distinguished as anything less than moral laws.

Using categories made by men infers those labels (such as "Hebraic" or "civil") are precisely correct. Using those labels to further categorize them as no longer binding places the authority in the man-made categorization, not their author, God. The only safe rule is that only those laws are changed which were fulfilled in the work of Jesus Christ (as described in Hebrews) or revised by apostolic authority elsewhere in the New Testament (as in Col. 2:16).

The law of God is God's rules of life. All of God's Word is His law, because it is all the command-word of our Sovereign, and God only speaks with absolute authority. Man cannot revoke God's Word by categorizing it or declaring it to be antithetical to His grace. The promise of God in Genesis 3:15 involved a guarantee of Satan's defeat and destruction. That was guaranteed at Calvary, where Satan's head was crushed, but it is applied to every sinner who turns to Jesus Christ when Satan's dominion over him is ended. Freed by the grace of God, the redeemed of Christ are now free of the curse, the death sentence of the law, and made new creatures to serve Him and to obey His Word, in newness of life.

Spheres of Influence

By Tim Yarbrough

"Our gracious Father, what a joy it is to serve Jesus Christ! We rejoice, O Lord, that this very earth is full of the mercies of our Lord. We're so thankful that when we wake up in the morning, we know that Thou art worthy to receive glory and honor and power, for Thou hast created all things, and for Thy pleasure they were and are created. Lord, we rejoice to know that He has ascended to the heavens and sits at the right hand of the Father, and that the Father said to the Son, 'Sit thou here until I make thy enemies thy footstool.'

"And Lord, we're thankful that we live in a world where the future of this earth is so bright and promising because the Word of the Lord and the knowledge of the Lord will cover this earth as the waters cover the sea. We ask as we think on these things that you will help us to be faithful stewards where You have placed us, to the glory and honor of the Lord Jesus Christ.
Amen."

One of my favorite passages is from Deuteronomy 5:29. In it, the Lord is speaking to Moses and says,

"If only they had such a heart to fear Me and keep all my commands always, so that they and their children would prosper forever."

The Lord Himself communicated that they would have a heart "to fear Me and keep My commandments."

In the book of Colossians there's a wonderful passage of scripture starting in chapter 1 verse 9:

> "For this reason also, since the day we heard this, we haven't stopped praying for you, asking that you may be filled with the knowledge of His will in all wisdom and spiritual understanding, so that you may walk worthy of the Lord, fully pleasing to Him, bearing fruit in every good work and growing in the knowledge of God. May you be strengthened with all power, according to His glorious might, so that you might have great endurance and patience, joyfully giving thanks to the Father, who has enabled you to share in the saints' inheritance in the light. He has rescued us from the domain of darkness and transferred us into the Kingdom of His Son He loves. In Him we have redemption, the forgiveness of sins."

Now, if we go to chapter 3 of Colossians, starting with verse 5, we find this:

> "Therefore put to death what belongs to your earthly nature: sexual immorality, impurity, lust, evil desire, and greed, which is idolatry. Because of these, God's wrath is coming upon the disobedient."

Now, that's an instructive principle.

> "And you were once walking in these things, when you were living in them. But now put away all the following: Anger, wrath, malice, slander, and filthy language from your mouth. Do not lie one to another, since you have put off the old self with its practices, and put on the new self. You are being renewed in the knowledge, according to the image of your Creator."

Here, we have instructions. God's desire for us as a people is that we would have a heart to fear him and that we would be willing to joyfully obey the Lord's commandments.

This morning, I'm going to relate a little bit of my story as a beginning Christian Reconstructionist, but my theme is prioritizing the Kingdom through understanding and maturing in your spheres of influence. If you– young men particularly– can grasp this at a young age, you won't waste the years that some of us wasted, inviting failure into our lives.

I'll explain what I mean by that, and I'm going to do it in this fashion: God has given to each of us "spheres of influence." He has also prioritized those spheres of influence. For instance, if you spend time around great Christian Reconstructionists for a while, you eventually become burdened with enormous problems, don't you? You start to realize that we have a nation that's in trouble! We have international problems, and these things are big and heavy! Then what invariably happens is that we focus on those things.

Take, for instance, the monetary problem. We have a problem with fiat currency, true. We have a problem with massive debt, while we have the elderly– the baby boomers– moving into their older years. Social Security and Medicare are reaching their limits sooner than they had anticipated in the last expert prediction, which was last year.

These are massive, huge problems because they're going to default!

But how many of you have been called from Washington and asked about how to solve the fiat currency problem? None! That's shocking, isn't it? How about the taxation problem? Have any of you been asked about how to solve it? Again none, which causes us to wonder, "Do we have any influence at all?"

With this in mind, for the next few minutes, I'd like to detail each "sphere of influence" that every one of us has.

The first sphere of influence for every individual is self-government. This is exactly what we were just reading about in the passage of Scripture above.

Our second sphere of influence is family government. It doesn't matter if you are a husband, a wife, a son, or a daughter; you are part of a family government.

Next is what we call our "intentional sphere of influence." This is so vital to our lives! This sphere of influence is the community where we live.

And in our particular social structure, the next sphere of influence is what we call the state, and then the federal, which make up the civil sphere.

All of those huge problems that I just talked about are located where? They're out here in the civil sphere, aren't they? And notice again that none of you people raised your hands about being called and asked how to address this stuff!

I can tell you, this has been a problem for me! I understood the money issues, I understood the tax issues, I understood the war issues– you know, how we go out and create wars! Now, I have invested a lot of time in every one of these areas. And guess what I have for it? I still have zero influence! I invest a lot of time where I have no influence, and yet I'm looking for a reward. But it never works out!

When we build our lifestyles around this– investing time where we have no influence– here's the one thing that we do accomplish: we ensure the defeat of our objectives! We intentionally court "losing"! When we court defeat, it's frustrating! We can't solve these problems, and nobody wants our input. We intentionally court areas where we have no influence and end up bringing our frustrations right back to our personal lives and our family's lives.

I cannot tell you how many times, over the course of the years, that I have witnessed this within the structure of a family. There's nothing worse than always hearing that we're losing, we're losing, we're losing... and yet it isn't true! We just read in the Scriptures that the wrath of God was on the disobedient. So while I have no influence in the civil sphere, I know who does– and God is judging him. If God is judging (and He is! I mean look at us, we're broke!) then we have some major changing to do!

Now, I'm just a country boy from Alabama. Years ago when the Lord converted me, I was very serious about my conversion. Because I thought my life should be committed to Christ, I actively went looking for mentors.

To give you just a little example of what happened, I was in a public high school, and before the teacher came into the science classroom one day, the Holy Spirit came into the room. Students were on their knees, crying and weeping! The whole room! God was granting repentance to a lot of students. The teacher– a professing Christian– walked in, and it scared her to death! We didn't know what was going on; we just knew our hearts were broken about our wickedness and our sins. So we went looking for mentors, but we couldn't find older men or women who were willing to be mentors!

At the time, I didn't understand it. But God used that in my life because I made a commitment that this same thing would never happen to a young person in an area where I was. That commitment led to the establishment of a mentoring and apprenticeship program where over the years we've had a little over four hundred young men, and women come through– primarily young men.

You learn a lot in being that close and mentoring that many young people. The first thing I learned is that too often we set our standards far too low in the expectations for young people in our culture. We tend to think, "It's taking them a while, but they'll get there, just given time." Instead, we ought to look them in the eye and tell them that they are to conduct themselves like they are ambassadors for a King! We ought to be telling them, "You are to be a young man of integrity and honor! You are to be trustworthy! You are to set an example for others around you!"

Our prayer for all of our kids comes from Psalm 144:12, and I have watched them exceed far beyond whatever we thought might be their service to Christ. Psalm 144:12 says, "…that our sons may be as plants grown up in their youth." Have you ever thought about that? When a plant is young, it takes life from all around it. Moms, isn't that how it works? The young just take life from you! They take their food from you; they take life.

But we pray that those plants will be grown up in their youth, which means as early as possible. Young men, you are to quit *taking* life, and you are to start *giving* life because that's what a plant does, doesn't it? It turns into food, turns into nourishment for everything around it. "That our sons may be as plants grown up in their youth." You become a "life-giver" in your youth.

And about our daughters this passage says, "That they may be like a cornerstone polished after the similitude of a palace." I wanted my daughter to know that God designed her to walk like a king's daughter! He intended that others would look at her as a king's daughter.

Sphere of Influence: Self-Government

Once when we were at Boy Scouts, there was a young man standing at the bottom of the stairs watching my daughter walk up the steps. He did not know me or my daughter. I walked up, put my arm around him and said, "Son, that looks good. But don't you touch."

Well, as you can imagine, the young man responded, "I-I-I wasn't looking!" I said "Son, it's too late to lie. You were locked in like a radar! And that's OK. I understand. God designed you to find women attractive. But it's what you do with it that's important. I'm thankful you find my daughter attractive. But you heard what I said, don't touch."

Now, I'm going to tell you a story about how I teach young people just like this young man how to exercise their first sphere of influence by learning to be self-governed. I often go out to parking lots and gathering areas where young people are, and I find that most of them are lost. They have all kinds of issues! Now, some people– particularly Christians– are kind of squeamish about sex, but I ask these kids, "Would you like to hear about sex in economics?" And boy, do they want to hear it!

So here's what I tell them: In the market place prior to 1952, there was a low supply of sex. When you have a low supply but a high demand, what happens to the price? It goes up! Back in that day, there was a high price to pay for sex: you had to get a job, you had to have some stability, and you had to be willing to marry the gal because there was a potential problem called "pregnancy." Because the consequences were high and the price was high, in 1952 birth control was introduced in this country.

When birth control was introduced, it was like Darwin's book in 1859 which sold out the first day! Birth control took off like a rocket and all of a sudden the marketplace experienced a significant increase in the supply of sex– and yet the demand didn't go any higher than it was before, because the demand on the part of the men was always at a peak.

So what happened? The supply went up, yet demand remained the same. And when that happens, what happens to the cost people are willing to pay for it? The cost goes down, and the women complain that "There are no good men!"

By this time in my story, my audience which is typically about fifteen to twenty young people, start to track.

By 1962– before any of these kids were born– the Supreme Court of the United States ruled in a case called Griswold versus Connecticut that it wasn't any business of the government to stick their nose into your bedroom concerning contraception. The legal restraints that had existed before were removed. It's not relevant to me whether you agree with or disagree with it; it's just the process from an economic standpoint.

This led to 1973 when that great supply that met the demand created yet another problem, and this thing called "abortion" was introduced. Abortion was an economic factor in order to eliminate the consequences of supply-demand choices. (As I'm explaining this to the young people that gather to hear, at this point they get it!)
Then, with Obergefell there was an even greater supply of sex on the market place. It was just all over the place!

So then I ask the question to the ladies, most of them aged 16 to 22, "Do you feel the pressure on you to participate in sexual activities? Do you feel like you must be the guardian of sexual activities?" What do you think they say? Every gal says, "Yeah!"

So then I ask the guys, "Now, what you think about that? Isn't that the way it works?" That's exactly what happens! "But what if there was a system where the onus was not on the young woman? What if that system were to say that if a young man allows himself to seduce a young woman– or to be seduced by her– it would cost him three years of his wages, and it could be enforced legally? What do you think about a system like that?"

Inevitably, the guys say, "No!" While the gals say, "Oh, yeah!"

When I address these young people, I especially want to address the young men because they are the responsible parties under God's law. Young men, it is on you to maintain a standard of godly sexuality in the culture in order to honor Christ!

To explain this to young men requires integrity. They can no longer look at a young woman and expect to use her to satisfy their lust. They're going to have to have a different view of that young woman than one who's willing to be "used." I can't tell you how many times I've had young men confess things to me after I explain this idea in terms of economics, and I tell them, "You realize you have to straighten this up!" And then we go through the process.

I share this story with you so that as Christian young men, you assume the integrity of a plant growing up in its youth, that you will institute a culture of respectability. Women who don't respect that will not be attracted to you; they will try to seduce you. When you set a standard that brings a different level of ethics into a culture, people will try to portray you as a hypocrite in order to justify whatever it is they want to do.

You young men have a tremendous challenge. It's not one that hasn't existed for six thousand years! It has. It's a question of whether or not you have a heart to obey God, and set that standard high. And in our circle of influence here, this is what we do.

Sphere of Influence: The Family

For this discussion right now, we're going to get rid of the outer circles [i.e., state and federal government] because, for purposes of covenantalism, they're not important. They are absolutely irrelevant. It's not that they don't influence us, but they are irrelevant in our spheres of influence, and I'll show you why.

Often within the Christian Reconstruction circles, we criticize pietism, and then we lack piety. Sometimes we can be some of the most rude, crude, and unacceptable individuals that you will ever meet! I have been involved in Christian Reconstruction for better than thirty-five years, and many times I've seen that if you bite and devour one another, you destroy one another. Sadly, we've yet to learn the maturity of dealing with conflict with integrity.

What generally occurs is that we have a "what" and a "why" that we can all easily agree upon. What: the Kingdom of God. Why: because we're commissioned. But then when it comes to the "how," we disagree and are unwilling to let our brothers and sisters have flexibility in how they address these issues. If others don't align with my 'how,', I go after them, and we end up having no diversity! And yet "how" your family ought to be might be different from "how" my family ought to be. God gives us a framework, and there is variety within that. There are unique aspects to your family, and there are unique aspects to mine.

One of my own family's particular aspects is that as my children got older, I told them that we would practice communism until the age of 12. Then at the age of 12, we were going to become a free enterprise system. My children could practice "from each according to his ability, to each according to his needs" until age 12. Obviously there were some incremental exceptions, but at age 12, that stopped. At age 12, they became responsible for working and saving their own money, and they were responsible for providing all their extracurricular activities– their shoes, sports equipment, whatever. They were cut loose.

Now I have a son who's birthday is August 31st. The year he was 11, I was a basketball coach of the homeschool operation that we'd started in North Alabama. My son came to his mother and me on a Saturday morning on the 1st of August– and remember, he was 11 years old. Guess what was going to happen in 30 days? He would no longer get to be a communist!

So my son said, "Mom and Dad, I think this year if I could get my shoes early and get in four extra weeks of practice, that it would be such a great help to me."

I said, "Son, that is such a fantastic idea." Meanwhile, my wife was squeezing my arm like you would not believe! I said, "Let's eat breakfast and then go to the shoe store." So we ate breakfast, and we headed into town to the shoe store.

At the store, my wife and I went right over to the $39.99 and $49.99 shoes, but we looked around, and we couldn't find our son. Eventually, we did locate him in the $100-$120 shoes where our son gave us a 15-minute spiel on how the quality of these shoes is so fantastic that they are worth the price difference. So I said, "Great. Pick out the shoes you want."

For the first and only time in my life, I spent $100 on a pair of tennis shoes. My wife couldn't believe it, but I said, "Just be patient."

So my son was no longer a communist the next year. He was a working member of the free enterprise class. The next year on the first Saturday of August, I said, "Son, your idea last year was so fantastic." And at that age, shoes do not last two years. The boy is growing. "So after breakfast, let's go to the shoe store, and you can get your pair of shoes and get that extra four weeks of practice in."

We went to the shoe store and of course, his mother and I– having been educated the previous year about shoes and how they work– were over in the $100-$120 shoes. We looked around, and guess what we can't find? Our son! This year, we found him over in the $39-$40 shoes. And this year, my wife and I got a lecture about how the quality of these shoes has so improved, it's ridiculous to spend that amount of money on a pair of tennis shoes! Now he understood the difference between paying for what he worked for and what was essentially free money.

As our children grew up and prepared to leave home, this was an important conversation in terms of family dynamics. We sat down with each of our children and their future spouse and said, "What we want to make sure that we're very clear on how covenantalism works from an economic perspective. I figure that for the most part, you guys will handle the sex issue pretty well for the first year at least. After that, you might want to have a conversation about it. But from an economic perspective, here's how this works:

"When you leave home, you're going to be a separate unit, and you're going to make your own decisions. If you go out and you do stupid stuff, and you find that you're in need of help from your mom and dad, you are to bring your checkbook. If we go through your checkbook and discover that you've done stupid stuff, we will tell you that the answer is no. We will not do such a disservice to you as to remove from you the pressures that God brings to you in order for you to understand the value of God's economic system in your economic choices. Not going to happen.

"Now, on the other hand, if you have something that happens to you like an illness or a car wreck or a job loss, something that's beyond your control, that's a great indicator from the Lord to us that the resources that He's given us are intended to help you."

My children have grown up in a debt-free home. And, sure enough, all of them married, and they all decided to experiment with a different economic philosophy. They all came back to ask for counsel. But guess what did not come with them? The checkbook! You see, I did not have to decide for them. I didn't have to say one single word. They had already determined, "We don't need to take the checkbook because this was obviously dumb and stupid. Dad has already told us that he isn't going to give us any relief from it, so we're going to get some counsel on how to overcome the mistakes that we made. But we're not going to overcome the mistakes at dad's expense."

That's absolutely correct.

Now, in our growth as Christians and Christian Reconstructionists, God put the elders in place in our communities for a reason, just like in Ephesus. And He has put you where you are for a reason. I now understand that I'm not going to change the world. I used to think I could until I realized how big it was, and it was such a heavy burden to carry.

So in my first sphere of influence—my self-government—there are certain things that God prioritizes for me. Number one is the fact that He made me male. We do not have problems in our household distinguishing that. No one's confused. I'm a male. I'm also a husband, and no matter what happens in the rest of the world, I am commanded by God to be faithful in that relationship, am I not?

"Tim Yarbrough, you are to love your wife as Christ loved the church and gave Himself for her."

Sadly, I cannot tell you how many Christian Reconstructionist husbands I have seen– and I deal with marriage counseling all the time– that are professing Christian Reconstructionists, and yet the first law they violate is God's law regarding their wives. They're great on capital punishment but pathetic on loving their wives. Sound familiar? But which one of these laws is closer to us?

"Tim Yarbrough, you are to dwell with your wife in understanding. You are to honor her as the weaker vessel. These are the things that you are to do to your wife." That's God's law, is it not? We fail to obey it, and yet we believe that our great claim to fame, as it were, is that we love God's law.

I was in a counseling session this week with a professing Christian Reconstructionist and his wife. And there were some differences between them. Ten times in the course of just a few minutes, this husband interrupted his wife to correct her view of what she sees. Now if he does that in front of me, what do you think goes on at home? He's unwilling to listen to her! It doesn't matter if he thinks she's right or wrong, it's her view of things. And if you're going to live with your wife in understanding, guess what you have to do? You have to understand her! You have to understand her view!

We have to start here, in the first circle of influence, with our own self-government and with applying God's law from the inside, out. We can't just give lip service to it. My wife ought to feel like she is the most cherished woman walking on earth. And yet, back when I was focusing on the outer circles where I had no influence, the tendency was that I brought that frustration into my home, and consequently my wife felt neglected. She felt like she wasn't as important– and the reality was, that was true because I prioritized the wrong things.

God gives me a priority and the reason that He gave me a mate was so that it would be a training ground for applying the Law of God in very specific details. So then, my marriage leads me into the next sphere of influence–family government. My relationship with my wife – if I do it right and honor the Lord–will be my greatest influence in life! But if I cannot influence my wife for the Kingdom of God, the idea that I'm going to go out into the world and influence it for the kingdom of God is a joke. But worse than that, it's a lie.

So then I look at my influence in family government; that is, my children. The Lord instructs me, "Tim Yarbrough, you should be working so that those young sons can become plants grown up in their youth. Tim Yarbrough, you are to raise your children in the nurture and the admonition of the Lord."

Is that not God's law? It is! It's applied law. When you rise up in the morning, when you lay down at night, as you're walking by the wayside, when you're sitting in the backyard, when you're feeding the animals– in everything you do you with your children, you are to be instructing them into the law of God.

That's the law, isn't it? That's God's law applied. My children and grandchildren should be hearing from Grandpa and Dad every single day. "When we woke up this morning, did you know that it was God who gave you sleep? The Scripture says 'Lo, He gives His beloved sleep.' That's a law! That's the law of God!"

We are to raise our children and help them find the vision, the mission. Young people– young men in particular– there's a reason to bear patiently and pray for your parents! I'm not kidding about this. We laugh at it, but all dads know that this is true. Oftentimes, we can be so critical of our children that we forget the impact of being negative with them. We forget that they love to be encouraged. Sometimes we need help with that.

Once, I lost my temper with my son, and it's probably one of the most shameful incidences of my parenting. At 12 years of age, he loved to go out and swing an axe, and he would do it all day long, splitting wood for the wood heater. So I gave him an instruction and then went off to a really important business meeting that just turned into a disaster.

When I came back, I looked at what my son had done with the firewood, but it wasn't what I had told him to do. I got angry and said to him, "Why didn't you do what I said?" He looked at me and said, "But Dad, I did."

Now, immediately the Holy Spirit began to convict me, but why let that get in the way of a good spanking? So I spanked my son. The whole time I was spanking my son, I was being convicted that I was doing something wrong. I had lost my self-government. I was no longer being a father to him per the calling of God.

When I finished, and he was crying, I went for a walk around the field. I was drenched with conviction, and I didn't like it, because I'm a dad, and I had given a command that ought to have been followed. But I couldn't get away from it. So finally, I went back in, sat down, and said, "Son, would you mind telling me what you heard?"

And he repeated to me word for word what I said. I asked, "What did that mean?" My son took me outside and gave me a demonstration of what I had said to him. And I realized that the problem was not my son. Dad had given some instructions that were very clear in Dad's mind but understood very differently by my son.

So the Lord broke me, and I started crying. I said, "I'm so sorry! I've created such an injustice to you! This was so wrong. This was sinful conduct."

Now I had just beat the soup out of this boy, and yet my 12-year-old son got up, came over, and said, "Dad, it's okay." I don't think he could have said anything that would have been more heartbreaking. It was horrible! I had done such an injustice.

I share this with you because my son is nearly 40, and four years ago at Thanksgiving we were sharing things we're thankful for like we always do. I shared this story and how God has used it over and over through all these years to remind me of what a lack of self-government would do in harming other brothers and sisters. I mean, if I've done it to my own kids, I could likely do it to you, because you're not a precious to me as they are!

My son was sitting there in the living room, and he said, by God's mercy, "Wow, Dad! I don't even remember that!" That was as hard for me as his saying, "Daddy, it's okay." All these years, he had not carried that memory with him. I had. I wonder who that lesson was for? It was for Dad!

So the government of our own homes is the place where we should have the greatest amount of influence. We prepare our arrows in the context of our homes, and we influence them for good, for Christ, for his Kingdom. We encourage them to have a vision.

Proverbs 24:16 says,

"Though a righteous man falls seven times, yet will he rise again." Many times, I've asked young men this question: Why does he get up the seventh time?" Because all the quitters quit at one or two! By the time they get to three or four, they are learning the discipline of God's training. Here's how James (1:3) puts it: "Brothers, count it all joy when you come up against different trials, knowing this, that the trying of your faith is intended to create patience, and patience will create maturity." Patience will create experience, and experience will create hope, and hope will make you not ashamed.

When our kids fail, we ought to help them learn how to get up, because that's where their strength is going to come from! By the time they get to six or seven falls, people have gathered strength and confidence in what God is doing in their lives.

This is true all around us. Even with our wives, this is true. Even with us, this is true. Now we can start looking forward to our kids "getting up." But the direction that they fall in is what's important. Are they falling forward, or backward? We oftentimes confuse "direction" with "perfection." None of our children are going to get to perfection, just like we are never going to get there! But the remarkable thing is that if they're falling in the right direction, God is going to train them just like He trained you, and me, and the generations behind us, and the generations in front of us.

We want to help our children have a vision. Teach them, train them to make decisions using God's principles. In my home, we would take a notebook and have our kids write the entire book of James by hand. It's one of the great lessons we learned over the years. I think this is important in the training of your families, and also if you're starting to mentor, or if you're building a business. Then you must pull out of it lifestyle ethical lessons, be willing to explain those, and then work on a program asking, "How does this affect your life?" From there, we go to the book of Proverbs, and again, they have to copy it out by hand. No shortcuts.

The first lesson we want every young person to get is this: Every man is tempted when he is drawn away by his own lusts (James 1:14). Not when Satan comes at him. You have to own that because the first step to maturity is being responsible.

I want my sons to understand this. I want my daughter to understand this. You are tempted because of the remaining corruption within your nature. So here's how we normally play this out:

"You made me angry." Is that true? No, that is not true. It is not possible for him to make me angry. Anger is a choice.

"You frustrated me." Is that possible? No. I have to make a choice to be frustrated.

"Every man is tempted when he is drawn away of his own lust and enticed." Now whatever you did was an enticement. He did something, and it was an enticement, but what we do is shift the responsibility from our own nature to someone else's actions. In other words, we convert the enticement into the foundation of the problem. Do you see it? I bet you've done that more than once! And the problem that we have is exactly the same in our society.

So if you own that this is how it works and that you are responsible, then there are only three areas of life that you must be responsible in. In everything else, you can do what you want to. But there are three areas that you must assume responsibility for: that is, for every thought, every word, and every deed. Beyond that, you can do what you want.

You must own responsibility. In our homes, that must be a conversation piece because if you and I can get away from shifting responsibility, we will! In this process, there must be a conversation in our homes. "Dad is responsible for dad's thinking. Dad is responsible for the words that come out of his mouth, and for his conduct."

And it's through that that we have influence. If our children can learn to be responsible, the impact of sending out responsible individuals who aren't looking to convert enticements into the foundations of their issues is incredible.

So this is where we invest our time, and with the time investment, our influence increases. When I move from my wife to my children, what happens to the time that I can invest? It's going to go down a little bit.

Intentional Influence

The next circle is our intentional influence. These are the people we intentionally choose. Think about Psalm 1, "Blessed is the man that walks not in the counsel of the wicked, nor stands in the way of sinners, nor sits in the seat of scoffers." Think about Proverbs 13:20, how "a companion of wise men will be wise, but a companion of fools will be destroyed."

We intentionally select people who are going to be in this circle, those we call our intentional circle of influence. It's okay to say to someone, "You cannot be involved in the circle of influence here because this circle is going to impact my family. And I want wise people in this circle of my life because I want to interact with wisdom, discipline, and people who are lovers of Christ. I want my children to see that."

You pick these friends very carefully. Now here's the thing: In this circle of influence, you are either going to pick them, or they are going to pick you. Who do you want in control of that process? Either I am going to get to choose who gets to impact my family, or they're going to choose for me.

For instance, I might have seven friends in my intentional circle. It's not even possible for me to invite everybody from our local congregation into that circle, is it? There are people within our local congregations that I don't want in that circle. It's okay for me to tell them why, but Facebook isn't the best place to do that. I want to help them. I want them to become wise people. Right now they're not wise, but I want them to get there.

When I move out into that circle, notice that I have less time and less influence.

Sphere of Influence: the Community

This next circle of influence is the local community. As difficult as it is with growing families, it's very difficult to create cohesion and security and purpose, isn't it? It takes time, effort, energy, and planning. So I move out into my community, which is where the other homeschool groups and churches, social organizations, and businesses are.

They're all out here in this local circle. I can touch them, taste them, feel them. You know, there is no such thing as a "Facebook community." It does not exist. A community is people who share the walk of life together. You cannot share the walk of life with people on Facebook. It doesn't happen.

In the community, we have all these organizations. These people are important because leaven leavens slowly if it's effective. If we're going to impact our local culture, we need all these people functioning, creating their own third circles out here all over the place. That needs to happen, and it needs to be intentional. This is why we're doing it.

We move out into these circles, for instance, with our jail ministry or ministry to widows, or what we're doing in terms of our local commissioners and civil officials. We can gripe all we want to, but unless we give them a different paradigm to think from, and show them how God's Word brings liberty, showing them how to become lovers of liberty, it doesn't matter. So we engage these people.

The Beauty of Working Within the Proper Spheres of Influence

Here's the beauty of working within these spheres of influence. For one, I'm not carrying the weight of the world on my shoulders. The burdens I carry, I can touch, I can taste, I can see. In our community, a 29-year-old woman walked into the woods recently and blew her brains out. In our community, a 55-year-old mother drove her car into the forest and took her own life. I mean, I'm in a local community!

Within all of that, this is where we work to build influence. So if I want to change these outer circles –i.e., state and federal spheres– what do I change? I work at changing these first circles– myself, my family, my local community– right here! That's how we build, and that's how God prioritizes our lives. We can learn to give ourselves to this in terms of how we prioritize what we do, and it's okay to do that. It's certainly consistent with God's program without carrying the weight of the world on your shoulders because you and I are not capable of it. But when you can keep your spheres of influence small enough so you can learn to rejoice in it, it makes a huge difference.

I've just given you the whole first year of our apprenticeship program in 60 minutes. The idea is to make it realistic in terms of how we build our testimony and our reliability.

I'll end with this. Our goal is to be the most trustworthy people anyone ever meets. I ask the question often, "Why should anybody listen to you or to anything you have to say?" The standard response is, "Because I'm telling the truth." Well I have 200 churches in my community, and guess how many of those preachers will tell me the same thing?

"Trust" is a future expectation built on past performance. Jesus Christ put it this way: "He that is faithful in little (past performance) will be faithful in much." When my grandson says to me, "Grandpa, don't you trust me to do this?

"Well, no, I don't."

"Why not? I'm your grandson!"

"That's why! I know what your past performance is, and therefore I don't trust you for the future."

For for people in our communities, and for us, that's the way it is for. We must be people whose past performances create future expectations of excellence in our lives toward them, and for them.

Let's pray:

> *"Our gracious Father, help us to realize that He who has begun a good work in us will perform it until the day of Jesus Christ and that the Word of God that He sends forth to us will perform exactly what You intended to perform. I pray that you would bless my brothers and sisters here, that You would cause them to honor Your priorities and Your circles of influence that You've given them. Cause them, O Lord, to flourish like well maintained olive*

trees. Give them much and abundant fruit for the cause of Christ and His Kingdom. Amen."

PLOWING IN HOPE

By Rev. Michael Kloss

"Does he not certainly speak for our sake? It was written for our sake, because the plowman should plow in hope and the thresher thresh in hope of sharing in the crop." -1 Cor. 9:10

In commenting on this passage, Calvin wrote, "It is an unjust thing that the husbandman should lay out his pains to no purpose in plowing and thrashing, but that the end of his labour is the hope of receiving the fruits. As it is so, we may infer that this belongs to oxen also, but Paul's intention was to extend it farther, and apply it principally to men. Now, the husbandman is said to be a partaker of his hope when he enjoys the produce which he has obtained when reaping, but hoped for when plowing."

Clearly, a man ought to enjoy the fruit of his labor. A man ought to taste that object of his hope by which he derived the strength to labor. The Law of God states this plainly in Deuteronomy 20:5-7.

A man plows in hope. A man buys a field in hope. A man takes a wife in hope, and it is good and right that the the man should enjoy the object of his hope. He should not be prevented from doing so. A man labors in the hope of a consummation of his labor.

Jesus says we must not fear the world, for He has overcome it. He says all authority in heaven and earth are His. Therefore, we go forth on the Great Commission mission. That is that hope under which we labor, that Jesus has overcome the world!

Jesus has all authority in heaven and on earth. He stands victorious over His enemies. This is the meat and drink of heaven– the wedding feast of the Lamb– that we already participate in weekly at the Lord's table. We eat the first fruits of the harvest to come, the harvest that has already begun! Jesus was raised from the dead as a sign and seal of our rising from the dead. Our Hope is Jesus– His Lordship and victory, and we participate in this Hope as co-heirs. That is why we plow!

If our Hope is Jesus, do we hope in vain? If our Hope is Jesus, do we not have reason to boldly and confidently anticipate the fruit of such Hope? The fruit of God's final harvest is so abundant that the church militant is fed from just the first fruits.

Romans 8:32 says, *"He who did not spare his own Son but gave him up for us all, how will he not also with him graciously give us all things?"* Postmillennial eschatology is not merely a set of doctrines. It's an eschatology of dominion! It's an eschatology of hope for every sinner! It's the way, the truth, the life– for the whole world. If God the Father gives us the most valuable thing that ever came into this world– His beloved Son–how could He withhold *anything*?

Postmillenialism is not about a specific chronology of events. It's not about some distant, hazy future. It's about how you put your socks on in the morning. It's about how you change diapers, what you read, and how you read. It's about the alarm clock, and debit card, and your commute, and work, and curriculum, and the midterm elections.

Heaven has invaded earth! The glorious future of Heaven's eternal reign of joy has invaded the present, has invaded your heart by the Holy Spirit.

Right now, I want you to set your circumstances aside. Set current events aside. Set aside your angst and anxiety and fear. Set aside all that is present and carnal and temporary. Fix your eyes on the Victorious King– the Light of the world, and what He has promised.

The Grace of God has Appeared

Titus 2:11-14 says,

> *"For the grace of God has appeared, bringing salvation for all people, training us to renounce ungodliness and worldly passions, and to live self-controlled, upright, and godly lives in the present age, waiting for our blessed hope, the appearing of the glory of our great God and Savior Jesus Christ, who gave himself for us to redeem us from all lawlessness and to purify for himself a people for his own possession who are zealous for good works."*

God's gracious salvation has risen, and climbs higher and higher in the sky. We stand in its life-giving light, and yet we wait for the appearing of the glory of our great God and Savior, who gave Himself to redeem us from lawlessness. We await the full revelation of God's victorious Son, the full zenith.

The light of the gospel– the grace of God, the Son of God, the LORD Jesus– is bringing every human heart into submission to His law, and is working through His people to transform the world. We zealously work as the sunlight of Christ spreads to cover everything, beginning in our hearts and spreading to our every action outward until the full light of Christ drives all darkness out of the world– the full revelation of Christ's victory over everything.

A fish doesn't know that it's wet because it lives in the water. A fish knows only water. Likewise, it's hard for us to comprehend the light of Christ's victory for the same reason. It touches everything! We need to step out of it by the means of our imaginations to appreciate that we stand in the growing sun at the midmorning of history, and all around us is truth, beauty, and goodness.

In your wife's smile and in the laughter of her babies, in payday and peanut butter, at funerals and football games, in the aches and pains of age and the horror of cancer, in holocaust and holy war, we plow in hope. It's lighter out than an hour ago because we stand in the growing light of the Day of the Lord. We will sit at the high feast of Jesus and taste the fruit of our hope– we do every Sunday already– because our enemies around about the communion table are defeated by the Lamb of God.

We put our hand to the plow and don't look back. While it is day, we work. And it is *always* day, for the Light of the World has risen! As God's people, we need to understand three things: we need to understand that our hope is Jesus; that we are His plowmen; and that we will participate with Him in His glorious harvest.

Jesus is Our Hope

In his crucial book, *Paradise Restored,* Chilton wrote that, "the Bible gives us hope, both in this world and the next. The Bible gives an eschatology of dominion, an eschatology of victory. This is not some blind 'everything-will-work-out-somehow' kind of optimism. It is a solid, confident, Bible-based assurance that before the second coming of Christ, the gospel will be victorious throughout the entire world."

Philippians 2:9-11 says:

> *"Therefore God has highly exalted him and bestowed on him the name that is above every name, so that at the name of Jesus every knee should bow, in heaven and on earth and under the earth, and every tongue confess that Jesus Christ is Lord to the glory of God the Father."*

One day *everyone* will acknowledge the Lordship of Jesus–every tongue, and every knee. But we don't see that yet. The current reality is that Jesus is given the name above every name, but the reality of universal recognition is something we await.

"The essential quality of hope is that it is oriented to something in the future that one expects, but does not yet possess (Romans 8:24-25.)" This orientation begins with Jesus. He is Lord of heaven and earth, and though many do not acknowledge Him as such, God the Father has bestowed upon Him the name above every name, so that everyone will bow to, and serve Him. The same tension found here is also found in the Titus passage. Jesus is Lord, and yet many do not acknowledge His Lordship. So the reality of the Gospel confronts the myth of the nightly news, the bad exegesis of biblical prophecy, the man-centered pessimism, and rank unbelief of this world.

But Jesus *is* LORD!

All authority in heaven and earth are His (Matthew 28:18.)

Ephesians 1:20-22 affirms that God:

> *"...worked in Christ when he raised him from the dead and seated him at his right hand in the heavenly places, far above all rule and authority and power and dominion, and above every name that is named, not*

*only in this age but also in the one to come. And he
put all things under his feet and gave him as head
over all things to the church."*

All things are under His feet. All rule and authority and
power are Christ's, whether everyone recognizes it or not!

So we find ourselves in the wood between worlds. We find
ourselves in the age of Resurrection– where dying and rising
again are every day realities. Jesus was raised as the first
fruits, so that we would know the harvest is coming (I Cor.
15:23.) The sun is risen, yet it has not yet reached its zenith.

So we struggle here in the midst of Jesus' conquest. We
gather around His table of victory set amidst His enemies.
At times, it's hard to imagine Jesus is winning, I know.

Jesus' promises to us now are as if a historian were to walk
up to a paratrooper in Normandy on D-Day plus three,
embracing the trooper, congratulating him on his victory
over Nazism. The paratrooper would call the historian a
madman! Even the foxhole after the decisive battle is still far
from hearth and home!

Jesus declared, "It is finished!" The decisive battle was
fought by Jesus in the wilderness with Satan after His
baptism, on the cross of Calvary, and under Calvary in
Joseph of Arimathea's tomb that now stands empty. The
decisive battle occurred, and Jesus won– but He is still
cleaning up, and the last enemy to go down will be death
itself. Jesus defeated the General, and is working His way
down to the last private.

We know it's true. But this feast of promise is set amidst
those very enemies He is mopping up, who refuse to accept
that the war is ultimately over. Jesus turned the tide on D-
Day, but we still yearn desperately for VE-Day.

That is our Hope– the consummation, the final revelation, the moment when everyone everywhere recognizes what we know by God's grace, that the carpenter's Son, born in a Roman province, who was unjustly executed, was exalted to the right hand of God the Father as the Emperor of heaven and earth.

But the consummation of this reality still lies in the future. That is our hope. We live in an expectation of future events. Now, we have the daily task of believing the truth while we struggle with the falsehoods of the IRS, the overbearing boss, the atheist family members, hell bound and hostile. We hope. The abortion mills don't have the final word on the definition of murder.

As we look out on this world and address the overwhelming tasks of mother, breadwinner, businessman, public servant, homeschooler and homemaker, we have to remember what Rushdoony said that, "Nothing can be understood in the terms of itself or the moment, but only in terms of God."

He is the Light of the World

Jesus said that He was the Light of the World– not the light of believers, but the Light of the World– and that light is the life of men (John 1.) As we read in Titus, the salvation of the world is understood as a sun rising. In Isaiah 9:6-7 the promises of Messiah are formulated to give this metaphor real power. Christ's Kingdom here shall increase and have no end. Matthew connects this passage directly to Jesus. Isaiah 9:2 is quoted directly in Matthew 4:16.

John the Baptist's father, Zechariah, understood the Messiah's Lordship as a spreading, enveloping light. Luke 1: 78-79 records, *"because of the tender mercy of our God, whereby the sunrise shall visit us from on high to give light to those who sit in darkness and in the shadow of death, to guide our feet into the way of peace."*

The light of this world, the understanding –that by which we see and comprehend all things– is not the nightly news, not political hucksters, climate-change pseudo-scientists, or so-called Christian prophets who couldn't exegete their way out of a paper bag. The light of the world is Jesus!

This metaphor carries a lot of freight! Jesus is light. The Sun of Righteousness has risen! So what does light do? What does the *sun* do? Eschatology is not the overly complicated set of doctrines that so many have made it to be. It's hope for every person in their everyday life! Keep your eyes on Jesus. Consider what He calls Himself; the metaphor He uses from nature. Focus on Him, using that imaginative device. This way, you will draw hope from Him as you draw your every breath. No matter what happens in the world, look at Him as Rushdoony said.

The sun rises at morning and ascends. It climbs farther and farther into the sky as its light touches more and more. The sun's light reaches everything. The only reason there is darkness in the daytime is because something gets between a particular object and the sun, blocking the sun. During the day, clouds, buildings, trees etc. create shadow, but remove the object and the sun's rays touch everything.

Now if you hide in the basement of a crack house, the light of the sun can't touch you. There is a lot in the way. The spiritual example is as true as the physical example. Hiding in the moral basement of a moral crack house prevents the light of Christ from reaching you. The key is removing every conceivable obstacle and obstruction to the sun's light.

Unbelievers heap up obstructions to Christ's Lordship, thinking that they control the sun's ability to shine by hiding behind obstructions. When we remove every obstruction to

Christ's Light, His Lordship is seen to touch *every*thing. Now on a sunny day, someone can get an umbrella, or stand under a tree, but the sun is still there, shining brightly no matter what you try to put between it and yourself. Our mission is learning to say "No!" to unrighteousness, and "Yes!" to righteousness, to prevent obstructions between Christ's light and us. Enlivened by that Light, we are zealous for good works, letting that Light shine through us to those hiding behind obstructions to God's Light.

Fixing our gaze on Christ, the Light of the World, there is no room for darkness. Our Hope is true and powerful and pure because Christ's Kingdom is spreading, swallowing everything up as the light does the shadows. "The essential quality of hope is that it is oriented to something in the future that one expects, but does not yet possess (Romans 8:24-25.)

Hebrews 6:9-12 says:

> *"Though we speak in this way, yet in your case, beloved, we feel sure of better things– things that belong to salvation. For God is not unjust so as to overlook your work and the love that you have shown for his name in serving the saints, as you still do. And we desire each one of you to show the same earnestness to have the full assurance of hope until the end, so that you may not be sluggish, but imitators of those who through faith and patience inherit the promises."*

The evidence given for the author's confidence in the salvation of his readers is the good fruit of their service (work.) Paul is writing to saints who are laboring with faith, and that faithful labor is the assurance of the hope that holds firm to the glorious future of Christ's exaltation in every human heart.

John Piper also states, "Verse 12 implies that hope and faith are almost synonymous. Notice the connections: verse 11 says go hard after full assurance of hope; verse 12 says the result of that pursuit of hope is that you will be like those who through faith and patience inherit the promises. Pursue hope so that you can be like men of faith."

Keeping our eyes on Jesus, we see that the glorious reality in which we plough and struggle is the world in which Jesus has ascended to the right hand of the Father. The hope we have is the strength by which we work. Our Hope is why we are zealous.

Zealous for what? To work for the King as His plowman! The second thing we need to know is that...

We are Jesus' Plowmen

Our vocations fulfill the Cultural Mandate and the Great Commission. Every lawful calling from motherhood to medical doctor, from the home business to working for Amazon, is how the Sun is reaching behind and through every obstruction man can conceive of.

In Genesis 1:28:

> "God blessed them. And God said to them, 'Be fruitful and multiply and fill the earth and subdue it, and have dominion over the fish of the sea and over the birds of the heavens and over every living thing that moves on the earth.'"

In Matthew 28:19-20, we are commanded to:

> "...go therefore and make disciples of all nations, baptizing them in the name of the Father and of the Son and of the Holy Spirit, teaching them to observe

all that I have commanded you. And behold, I am with you always, to the end of the age."

"Fill the earth, subdue the earth, and have dominion over the earth." *Everything* is encompassed in that command. Likewise, "teach all the nations all the words of Jesus" includes everything. What's left out? Nothing! The command to rule, subdue, and fill the world encompasses everyone and everything. Every career and profession in which Christians engage is aimed at the advancement of Christendom. Christian blacks, Christian whites, Christian Asians, Christian Latinos, Christian cops, bankers, brewers, and framers, Christian wives, mothers, writers, sewers, bakers, lawyers.... I think you get it.

God's vision for His Kingdom coming on earth is bigger than anything we can imagine. And fixing our eyes on Christ, the Light and Life of the World, we have all we need to work faithfully to this end. Colossians 1:19-20 reminds us that:

> *"For in him all the fullness of God was pleased to dwell, and through him to reconcile to himself all things, whether on earth or in heaven, making peace by the blood of his cross."*

Colossians says that the cross is all about the harmonization of all things in heaven and on earth in Christ: man put right with woman, man put right with his enemies, man put right with his rulers, man put right with his work. How does the reconciliation of all things in Christ relate to law, architecture, construction, education, parenting, medicine, economics, bread-making, dressmaking, discipline, and infrastructure? To everything?

The Great Commission is our mandate for seeking the reconciliation of all people to God through Jesus Christ because the fall twisted us and our relationship with God. Broken and estranged from our mission to work in God's garden, fallen man pursues his own ends. The number of obstructions between men and the Sun of Righteousness are literally legion! Reconciled to the Father in Christ, man can pursue his created purpose of subduing, multiplying, and filling the world with Christ worshippers. Titus 2:15 reminds us that grace is training us to be godly and zealous workers.

The inclusivity of these commands means that every person– male and female, in every profession, socio-economic level, nationality, and geographic location– is called to faith in Christ.

The Cultural Mandate and the Great Commission are the general call to all of humanity. They are all-encompassing. Jesus is reconciling all things– all jobs, all workers, all people, all countries, all lands, all languages, whether in heaven or on earth– making peace through the blood of His cross. The sun climbs in the sky and touches everything, so we need to get everything out of the way of its life-giving light.

How does God reach into everything? He converts people in every conceivable profession. Ask yourself, what does a Christian engineer look like? Or a Christian accountant? A Christian carpenter? A Christian clerk? A Christian coder?

How does a Christian react to sin? To adversity? Tragedy? Triumph? To whom does a Christian give credit for blessing and for cursing? How does a Christian spend his money? How does a Christian treat his enemies and revilers? Does a Christian work to merely earn his pay? To serve himself?

How did the thief on the cross come to believe? Believing comes through hearing, but Jesus didn't preach a sermon to him. He prayed for and verbally blessed His persecutors, He gave the care of His mother to His friend John. Jesus on the cross, living faithfully unto death, was a Gospel demonstration that led the thief on the cross to faith. The thief *saw* the Gospel. The thief on the cross *heard* the implications of the Gospel. We think it's the job of professional ministry workers to spread a message of words, but the Good News is also a way, a life– not merely words.

God calls Christians into every conceivable lawful profession to bring about this grand plan one person, family, and profession at a time, reconciling all things in Christ. (Matthew 5:13-16.)

Chilton closes the first chapter of *Paradise Restored* with this passage, and the following summation:

> *"This is nothing less than a mandate for the complete social transformation of the entire world. And what Jesus condemns as ineffectiveness, failing to change the society around us. We are commanded to live in such a way that someday all men will glorify God– that they will become converted to the Christian faith. The point is that if the church is obedient, the people and the nations of the world will be discipled to Christianity. We all know that everyone should be a Christian, that the laws of institutions of all nations should follow the Bible's blueprints. But the Bible tells us more than that. The Bible tells that these commands are the shape of the future. We must change the world; and what is more, we shall change the world."*

One man, one profession, one family, one church at a time. One step at a time, one furrow at a time. Our hope is our strength, our confidence and our reason for plowing.

> *"For the grace of God has appeared, bringing salvation for all people, training us to renounce ungodliness and worldly passions, and to live self-*

controlled, upright, and godly lives in the present age, waiting for our blessed hope, the appearing of the glory of our great God and Savior Jesus Christ, who gave himself for us to redeem us from all lawlessness and to purify for himself a people for his own possession who are zealous for good works." (Titus 2:11-14)

Circumstances and current events often mislead and distract us. Take your eyes off the distractions and the lies that say we are losing! The sun rises and rises and no obstruction behind which people hide can diminish the power of the sun one bit. Remove the obstructions in your own life. Let the grace of Christ train you in righteousness, hoping in the consummation of Christ's Lordship so that you will zealously pursue good works, letting your light shine, demonstrating the love of God in your vocation.

You are a priesthood of believers. Like Adam, you were placed in the garden to be a priest-gardener, priest-mothers, priest-painters, priest-engineers, priest-students, priest-fathers, priest-doctors, priest-carpenters, priest-*[fill in the blank.]* Bookkeeping for a business is sacred work. Washing your family's clothes is sacred work. Designing a machine that functions well, just as your customer ordered it, is sacred work. Building cabinets, painting cabinets, filling those cabinets with food, using the contents of those cabinets to cook dinner... all of it is sacred work, if it is pursued for the glory of the Lord.

Colossians 3:23-24 says:

> *"Whatever you do, work heartily as for the Lord... You are serving the Lord Christ."*

Ecclesiastes 3:22 says:

"So I saw that there is nothing better than that a man should rejoice in his work, for that is his lot. Who can bring him to see what will be after him?"

Trusting in God's provision, trusting in God's promises of fruitfulness, looking to God to use our work for His glory, "the doctrine of vocation helps Christians see the ordinary labors of life to be charged with meaning. It also helps put their work into perspective, seeing that their work is not serving them, but that they are resting in the grace of God who in turn works through their labors to love and serve their neighbors."

God placed you in your current garden because of the people there, because there is opportunity to pursue His Kingdom goals there. These are opportunities for sanctification. You are sowing, weeding, watering, reaping right where God placed you, reconciling your days beneath the cross of Christ.

This hope gives us strength.

We Plow Because We Know that We Will Participate in His Glorious Harvest

God depends on us to be His hands, feet, and presence in the gardens of this world as His priest-gardeners! He expects us to plant, to build, to work. Our zeal and our hope is that we are working for God, and that we will participate in the harvest, reaping its plenty and blessing with God.

God created an interdependent universe. I can plant as many seeds as I desire, but I can't make it rain. God needs someone here to weed. God and man, building together.

Psalm 127:1 says, *"Unless the Lord builds the house, the builders labor in vain."* The Lord builds, and we build.

In John 4:33-38:

> *"The disciples said to one another, 'Has anyone brought him something to eat?' Jesus said to them, 'My food is to do the will of him who sent me and to accomplish his work. Do you not say, 'There are yet four months, then comes the harvest?' Look, I tell you, lift up your eyes, and see that the fields are white for harvest. Already the one who reaps is receiving wages and gathering fruit for eternal life, so that sower and reaper may rejoice together. For her the saying holds true, 'One sows and another reaps.' I sent you to reap that for which you did not labor. Others have labored, and you have entered into their labor.' "*

Here, Jesus is making a spiritual point using this creation order of interdependent work. One sows, and one enters that labor and reaps.

Jesus had just interacted with the woman at the well, doing the father's work of Messiah given to Him to do. The Samaritan woman seemed to have been given many elements of truth, which Jesus brought to fruition. Jesus, looking to the Father, entered the labors of sower and reaper, threshing the fruit from the chaff. This is our model. When you serve well, some of you plant seeds, some water, some weed, some reap– but God gives the harvest.

Our physical work has just such a spiritual dimension. Your vocation is part of God's remaking the world. Your vocation is how God is fulfilling the Cultural Mandate and the Great Commission.

I Corinthians 3:6-9 says:

> *"I planted, Apollos watered, but God gave the growth. So, neither he who plants nor he who waters is anything, but only God who gives the growth. He who plants and he who waters are one, and each will receive his wages according to his labor. For we are God's fellow workers."*

I Corinthians 9:10:

> *"Does he not certainly speak for our sake? It was written for our sake, because the plowman should plow in hope and the thresher thresh in hope of sharing in the crop."*

Titus 2:11-14:

> *"For the grace of God has appeared, bringing salvation for all people, training us to renounce ungodliness and worldly passions, and to live self-controlled, upright, and godly lives in the present age, waiting for our blessed hope, the appearing of the glory of our great God and Savior Jesus Christ, who gave himself for us to redeem us from all lawlessness and to purify for himself a people for his own possession who are zealous for good works."*

We look to Christ, hoping for the final revelation, hoping for the final judgment when all men are judged, and justice is meted out. We look to the harvest of the dead planted now as perishable seeds that will all rise in the final harvest unto eternal life.

We pray and evangelize, and preach and reconstruct this garden in faithful obedience to our Lord's commands, and there will be a day when all our labor and toil in this world will bear fruit, will explode with life eternal, when Jesus will judge the deeds and words of men.

A day is coming when clothed in Christ's Resurrection and Christ's Righteousness, we will see the reaper bringing in His sheaves. This is why we plow in hope.

Psalm 126:5-6:

> *"Those who sow in tears shall reap with shouts of joy! He who goes out weeping, bearing the seed for sowing, shall come home with shouts of joy, bringing his sheaves with him."*

Our hope in ploughing is participating with the reaper and thresher!

Think. Every man and woman will be raised. Whether they were righteous and redeemed, or not. God's love and grace means that every single person who ever lived will not stay dead. Jesus really will defeat, at the last, death itself for every human being. His life cannot be contained, and He is the life of the world.

John 5:28:

> *"Do not marvel at this, for an hour is coming when all who are in the tombs will hear his voice and come out."*

I Corinthians 15:51-55:

> *"Behold! I tell you a mystery. We shall not all sleep, but we shall all be changed, in a moment, int he twinkling of an eye, at the last trumpet. For the trumpet will sound, and the dead will be raised imperishable, and we shall be changed. For this perishable body must put on the imperishable, and*

this mortal body must put on immortality. When the perishable puts on the imperishable, and the mortal puts on immortality, then shall come to pass the saying that is written, 'Death is swallowed up in victory.' Oh death, where is your victory? Death, where is your sting?"

On the last day, the final revelation of Jesus is His final victory over all His enemies, and the last will be death– the harvest of every person who ever lived will come out of the ground and seas where they were buried. Jesus is the first fruits of the harvest of everyone who came from the womb. They will come again out of the womb of the world.

Between the first resurrection of Christ and the final resurrection of all men and women is the period in which we labor– the season in which we plow. And the harvest to come will not be universal salvation, but universal defeat of death because Jesus' life is so overflowing, and His victory so total that everyone will be lifted.

And in that harvest, Christ will winnow. Christ will gather His wheat, the body of Christ. The loaf of eternal communion will be gathered into God's barn. John 5:29 says:

"Those who have done good, to the resurrection of life, and those who have done evil, to the resurrection of judgment."

Romans 14:9:

"For to this end Christ died and lived again, that he might be Lord both of the dead and of the living."

The world will be saved from death, and upon that final consummation of victory, every tongue will confess and every knee will bow– Jesus is Lord. Then the wicked will be excommunicated from the world to eternal hellfire. God's grace is so overflowing that after He has defeated death for everyone, He will give everyone exactly what they wanted: eternal life with Him, or eternal life without Him. What a benevolent King!

And *you* will be there in the barn, with all the other wheat. You will see the fruition there of all your labors here. Everyone who rejects you rejects the One who sent you. Everyone who hears Christ's words and does not listen to His voice will go to a place where His voice cannot be heard. Every seed planted here, every weed ripped from the ground will be eternally dealt with. So, plough in hope! Everything you ever said and did will be judged. And Jesus, on the merit of His life, will pardon saint after saint after saint.

You will be there in the final harvest, together with the Bride of Christ beautified. Philippians 1:6 says, *And I am sure of this, that he who began a good work in you will bring it to completion at the day of Jesus Christ."*

Ephesians 5:25-27:

> *"Husbands, love your wives as Christ loved the church and gave himself up for her, that he might sanctify her, having cleansed her by the washing of water with the word, so that he might present the church to himself in splendor, without spot or wrinkle or any such thing, that she might be holds and without blemish."*

Romans 8:28-30:

> *"And we know that for those who love God, all things work together for good, for those who are called according to his purpose. For those whom he foreknew he also predestined to be conformed to the image of his Son, in order that he might be the*

firstborn among many brothers. And those whom he predestined, he also called, and those whom he called, he also justified, and those whom he justified, he also glorified."

What is our hope? That we have a faithful and trustworthy husband and LORD. You and I together, the Church Universal. He will present His Bride in splendor, completing through the washing of the word, our purification, sanctification–eternal splendor. And we will see all things work out for good. We will be glorified at Christ's right hand.

1 Corinthians 6:2-3:

"Or do you not know that the saints will judge the world? And if the world is to be judged by you, are you incompetent to try trivial cases? Do you no know that we are to judge angels? How much more, then, matters pertaining to this life!"

Saints, don't be caught napping! It's midday, and the sun rises higher and higher. The light of the world spreads, and it will touch everything, and at the harvest even the sun of this world will be unnecessary, for we will truly see the light of the world, the life of men, and all things reconciled in Him.

Revelation 22:3-5:

"No longer will there be anything accursed, but the throne of God and of the Lamb will be in it, and his servants will worship him. They will see his face, and his name will be on their foreheads. And night will be no more. They will need no light of lamp or sun, for the Lord God will be their light, and they will reign forever and ever."

This light shines forth now, it climbs higher and higher. Get everything out of its way! Remove every obstruction in your own life. Plow in hope. Be zealous for your work for the sake of the world, for it is the Lord's and the fullness thereof. All authority in heaven and on earth are Christ's, so fix your gaze on Him and plow in faith and hope!

2 Corinthians 4:1-6 says:

> "Therefore, having this ministry by the mercy of God, we do not lose heart. But we have renounced disgraceful, underhanded ways. We refuse to practice cunning or to tamper with God's word, but by the open statement of the truth, we would commend ourselves to everyone's conscience in the sight of God. And even if our gospel is veiled, it is veiled to those who are perishing. In their case, the god of this world has blinded the minds of the unbelievers, to keep them from seeing the light of the gospel of the glory of Christ, who is the image of God. For what we proclaim is not ourselves, but Jesus Christ as Lord, with ourselves as your servants for Jesus' sake. For God who said, 'Let light shine out of darkness' has shone in our hearts to give the light of the knowledge of the glory of God in the face of Jesus Christ."

Part II

Family Business

The Necessity of Family Business

By Joseph M. Graham

The family is the first institution created by God. When we talk about family business, this is the first thing we need to realize. The family is very, very important. It's the *family* that was tasked with taking dominion over all creation. At Creation, Adam was given a task, but he was incomplete. Therefore, he was given his wife, and together they were commissioned with executing the dominion task.

The family is responsible for education, welfare, property, childrearing, producing, and increasing. When you read the dominion task, those are all the things that God wants the *family* to do.

Cultivating Business Like We Cultivate Family

When learning about a family business, begin with any company in mind. Every business is tasked with the responsibility of maintaining production, of possessing property and selling it. They are concerned with educating customers and employees on their function and services. They want to meet market demands. A business is also concerned with being mature. Businesses don't want to be static; they want growth in their organization. They want to become competent and capable. A business is also concerned with increase, and expanding market share.

What does that sound like? It sounds exactly like what a *family* is supposed to do! Production, property, education, maturation, increase are the same areas in which the family is responsible. In his book *Family Wealth: Keeping it in the Family, How Family Members and Their Advisers Preserve Human, Intellectual, and Financial Assets for Generations*, James Hughes said:

> *"Families attempting long term wealth preservation often don't understand that they are businesses, and that the techniques of long term succession planning, practiced by all the other businesses, are available to them as well."*

James Hughes puts the cart before the horse, while God arranged life the other way around. In God's world *businesses* get their template from *the family*. I'm not sure of all Mr. Hughes's presuppositions, but he's still on the same general track. The Bible says that good businesses get their practices from the template of the family. Think about that.

Good businesses take their purpose much more seriously because they codify it. They formalize their mission and vision. They are serious about their function because they want their customers to know what they are about, and what can be expected. Families typically don't have that same mindset. We usually operate informally, just executing based on a vague idea of our mission and purpose. The family vision is not clear, so our goal isn't easily identified.

The mission of a family is also unclear, yet it's the family that is tasked with the primary dominion mission from God. What our families *need* is a clear mission. It needs to know *Where* it's headed, *what* it's doing, and *how* it expects to achieve those goals.

With that mentality, families will have the ability to grow in all these areas of dominion just like a well-organized business would grow.

If you were going to start a business or a brand from scratch, I recommend you listen to Michael Hyatt. He is excellent. Hyatt would explain that step one for your business is to establish your vision and mission. When the rubber meets the road and business operations struggle, you're going to need to refer back to your vision and to your mission statement. Every business will encounter obstacles and challenges, just like they do in a family. But the vision and the purpose are what help you navigate through challenges and difficulties, and will guide how to overcome those obstacles. Good families will operate in the same way.

The principles behind good businesses are drawn from relationships that undergird the family. Families that grow with an eye toward the collection of God-given assets naturally develop the cultivation of their own resources for its continued success. There are different visions for every family. Some are called to agricultural mindsets, some to the city, or some might be led to start a retreat center. It doesn't really matter what area the family is drawn towards. The point is that each family should be committed to the development of its own resources, which God has given to each family for their success.

In the *Family Wealth* book, Hughes tells a story about John D. Rockefeller, Sr., and a critical decision that was made concerning his only son, John D. Rockefeller, Jr. Rockefeller was a very successful entrepreneurial business tycoon in the oil industry. His business was doing very well developing precious commodities and earning a hefty profit in the process. Yet despite his success, Rockefeller Junior wasn't interested in the business career of his father. Hughes writes:

"An unrecognized part of the Rockefeller's success in long-term wealth preservation is the extraordinary act by John Davison Rockefeller, Sr., of not compelling his son to remain in the family business once he had determined that his calling lay in family governance and philanthropy. Here is America's wealthiest man, with only one son, agreeing that the son was no obliged to follow the father's dreams. I believe the father's willingness to free his son to follow his individual pursuit of happiness is one of the best long-term wealth preservation decisions in history. It is interesting that John Davison Rockefeller, Sr., continued for the rest of his life to do what he loved, thereby adding immeasurably to the family's intellectual and financial capital. It is also interesting that John D. Rockefeller, Jr., urged each of his children to find work that led to their individual pursuits of happiness. The resulting contributions of the third-generation Rockefellers to philanthropy, government, international banking, and investment in new industries are remarkable. Today, more than 120 years since the founding of the fortune, the Rockefeller family clearly understand that its wealth lies in its human and intellectual capital, and that its financial capital is a tool to enhance the pursuits of happiness of its individual members."

When my son Korbin was about ten years old, we were living in Mississippi. On his tenth birthday, I gave him a special gift. I was being influenced by men who encouraged viewing your children as future adults, and I wanted to give him a gift that was going to encourage him towards maturation, not towards continued childishness. I decided to give him a toolbox for his birthday: hammer, tape measure, nails, and screwdriver. He was ecstatic, which was a good sign to me! We took this tool chest and we built things together.

When I was young, I didn't grow up with a dad in the home. I came from a broken family without any day to day discipleship in manhood or what that meant. I certainly didn't know how to build anything! I'd never done it before, but that didn't stop me from trying to teach my son. I didn't care about what I didn't know. What I cared about was that I wanted to do something with my son, and I was willing to learn with him because it would benefit us both.

What we started out building was ugly. It wasn't very sturdy, pretty, or useful, but that didn't matter to me because I just wanted to show my son that we needed to learn things we didn't know how to do. Dads, we shouldn't be scared or intimidated about what we don't know. I was so naïve, I didn't even know about YouTube back then. We used books, and we built things together! Today, I am so proud of my son– he can build amazing things! He is more capable with tools than I am, and it makes me so proud. Pouring into him and encouraging him was worth all the effort. I knew he could do it. All that was needed was the vision and support.

Patiently Cultivating Success

Psalm 1 describes the man of God as being a fruit-bearing tree. Thinking about the cultivation of fruit trees, how is it done? You start with nothing. You have to "see" the tree before it exists. First, you need soil. Then you plant and water the tree. Then it takes time to grow. When you sit down and read your Bible in the morning, do you get growth and wisdom coming like lightning bolts from the sky, appearing suddenly, telling you precisely what you are to do? No! Growth doesn't happen that way. Like a growing fruit tree, it's a slow, steady process. We grow methodically, through daily disciplines over time, little by little; like water through rocks, we're shaped.

I encourage you to take time to develop and understand what a multi-generational distribution of wealth looks like. Consider these future assets as fruit trees that your family will possess and cultivate for their benefit. When planning for a developed orchard, you have to see it before it exists.

You don't just come into a fully mature garden and see fruitful trees the moment you want or need them. When we desire to have consistently producing trees, we have to understand they take time to develop. Our families, our children, and our assets are precisely the same. You will have to visualize their existence, and develop them through careful planning for future cultivation. It will take time, effort, and energy. But through the process, you must have a picture of the goal you are trying to achieve.

Truth is Truth

My son and I recently attended a conference on the east coast focusing on a business that we're getting involved in. Inside of this industry, they have what is called the "Millennial Movement." It's a brand inside the organization inspiring people to influence the next generation of millennials. It's very motivated, a little flashy, and they're doing well in the industry.

In this business, leveraging their influence, they are able to make money in that market space. At this conference, sharply dressed young men were talking about the specifics of the business, how they've found success, and the disciplines that helped them. But they readily admitted that they didn't have the character to handle the success they achieved. They may have made more money, but it merely created more of what was already there—deficiencies in character. They didn't have the character to manage the organizations they had built, and they crumbled. Over 80% of the time the speakers presented was devoted to discussing the importance of character!

These presenters were talking about truth. These secular people discussed the business law of attraction—that you attract people based on whom you spend your time with. I, of course, recognize this principle. The *Bible* says, "Whoever walks with the wise becomes wise, but the companion of fools will suffer harm." (Prov. 13:20) What they are talking about works because it is true! It doesn't matter what field you're in, truth is truth. They called it the "law of attraction," God calls it a Proverb. It's a principle of truth.

They said, "You need to be part of something bigger than yourself. If you know that you're a part of something bigger than yourself, it inspires you." These people were getting inspired about the potential future of their business because that are beginning to see possibilities that don't exist yet, which paint a bigger picture than they initially imagined. Yet, despite all of their imagination, they don't have anywhere near the blessings and promises that Christians have. They don't even see the Kingdom or posses the kinds of blessings we do,

> *"His divine power has granted to us all things that pertain to life and godliness, through the knowledge of him who called us to his own glory and excellence, by which he has granted to us his precious and very great promises, so that through them you may become partakers of the divine nature, having escaped from the corruption that is in the world because of sinful desire." (2 Pet. 1:3-4)*

Unbelievers are receiving inspiration that is driving them to work hard, and with fervency for a significant impact. One man said he started his business because he wanted to help bring dads home. I think that's a beautiful goal to strive towards. Wouldn't it be wonderful to be able to provide more men with the opportunity to work closely with their families and not have to be beholden to a "job" anymore!

Well, we can certainly do that. We can work with our families and with people that we love and care about. Look at the tools and resources we have at our disposal! Now, why am I talking about these ideas?

Cause and Effect

"Know therefore that the LORD your God is God, the faithful God who keeps covenant and steadfast love with those who love him and keep his commandments, to a thousand generations, and repays to their face those who hate him, by destroying them. He will not be slack with one who hates him. He will repay him to his face. You shall therefore be careful to do the commandment and the statutes and the rules that I command you today." (Deuteronomy 7:9-11)

All of life, including business, is about the covenant. God is covenantal. It's real, and there are effects associated with what we do and what we think. The covenant is alive, and the covenant creates inequality. The covenant disbars the idea that everyone is equal or is treated as such. This humanistic viewpoint is not going to happen because the covenant intrinsically creates separation between those in and those out. Those who don't comport with what the covenant says, and don't abide by its principles, are subject to inequalities. They're called blessings and curses. That's inequality. If you read Deuteronomy 28, it starts out very simply:

"If you fully obey the Lord your God and carefully follow all his commands I give you today, the Lord your God will set you high above all the nations on

146

earth. All these blessings will come on you and accompany you if you obey the Lord your God: You will be blessed in the city and blessed in the country. The fruit of your womb will be blessed, and the crops of your land and the young of your livestock — the calves of your herds and the lambs of your flocks. "

That is the marketplace. That is the home. That is the church. Men have not been made equal except in the requirement they have to believe and obey God.

The covenant includes law because *God* is about law. These are where we get the very principles by which we measure obedience and disobedience. This is easily understood and translated in the marketplace as well as in the community. The responsibility we assume as Christians is, therefore, to be the ones most in tune to the realities of God's covenant, to be obedient participants of it, and loyal advocates for it.

Since the truth of inequalities is based on the fruits of obedience and disobedience, then we should be excited to embrace and transmit the truths of God's system of economics, business, politics, family, government, and everything! To be truly wealthy: spiritually, physically, and materially, we have to be ones personally embodying the character, stewardship, and work of the anointed.

Dennis Peacocke in *Doing Business God's Way* explains it this way. We must "carry the following message:

*   To him who is faithful in managing what he has, God will give more.
*   God doesn't take from those who have in order to give to those who don't have.
*   God takes from those who don't practice good stewardship to give to those who do.

- God doesn't reward disobedience and punish obedience.
- God rewards good management, but poor management has its own negative consequences."

The development of a strong family business comes through covenants and law, both internally within the organization, and externally with how the family functions, to everybody outside. Obedience to covenantal ethics translates just as strongly in business practices as it does individually and in the family.

A Big Vision!

One of the men who spoke at the conference my son and I attended was John Gardner. The first thing John told us from stage was, "You are not thinking big enough!" And my mind just exploded! How big are you thinking about your family? How big of an impact can your family make?

If your family is going to be an influencer 200 years from now, what would you do today? What would you do differently today if that were where you knew you were headed? If you start a business, don't say, "I hope our business is going to be around in ten years." No! Instead, work and plan as if it's going to be around in a *thousand* years!

When Arthur Guinness opened up his brewery, he saw a social issue where he lived. He signed a lease for his building for nine thousand years! Why? Because he had a big vision for what he was building. He told himself, "I am building something that's going to last a long time." This affected the decisions and choices that he made. We need to have a big vision for what the purpose of our family enterprise is, and how broad its impact will be.

The book of Nehemiah records the story of how Nehemiah heard about what was happening to the walls and the city in Jerusalem. The first thing he did when he heard of the destruction was repent. He realized, "I need to change." When you see a problem, the first thing you need to do is ask, "How do I need to change? What do I need to do differently?"

Nehemiah stopped what wasn't working and went back to the Lord to understand what actually needed to happen. When Nehemiah's entire journey started, do you know what his vocation was? He was a bartender! A cupbearer to the King. He brought the King alcohol. Fifty-two days later, he rebuilt the entire walls of Jerusalem– and they'd been down for a hundred years!– because he had a vision of what he wanted to do, and he was able to do it. That's a big reason. He had a big vision, and he was able to make it happen.

We all know the story about the 12 disciples. Do you think they had a problem thinking big enough? No! They went about their work everyday understanding they were discipling the world. *Every*body! *Nobody* was off limits. Everyone in the entire world! The same Spirit that was in them is in us! We have access to the same power.

Acts 3:18-26 says:

> *"But what God foretold by the mouth of all the prophets, that his Christ would suffer, he thus fulfilled. Repent therefore, and turn back, that your sins may be blotted out, that times of refreshing may come from the presence of the Lord, and that he may send the Christ appointed for you, Jesus, whom heaven must receive until the time for restoring all the things about which God spoke by the mouth of his holy prophets long ago.*

"Moses said:

> *'The Lord God will raise up for you a prophet like me from your brothers. You shall listen to him in whatever he tells you. And it shall be that every soul who does not listen to that prophet shall be destroyed from the people.' And all the prophets who have spoken, from Samuel and those who came after him, also proclaimed these days.*

> *"You are the sons of the prophets and of the covenant that God made with your fathers, saying to Abraham, 'And in your offspring shall all the families of the earth be blessed.' God, having raised up his servant, sent him to you first, to bless you by turning every one of you from your wickedness."*

The disciples were talking about things that needed to happen based on what God had been doing in history. They understood that God's promise is now being fulfilled. They looked back in history and saw that everything that had happened led up to *this moment*. All the prophecies, history, and the prophets came to *that moment*, and they've fallen upon their heads! And then it clicked, and they said, "This is what needs to happen."

Mr. Rushdoony, in his essay, told us about Christian Reconstruction and what it means. This is how I would explain it:

> *"For the creation waits with eager longing for the revealing of the sons of God. For the creation was subjected to futility, not willingly, but because of him who subjected it, in hope that the creation itself will be set free from its bondage to corruption and obtain the freedom of the glory of the children of God."* (Romans 8:19-21)

This is how I understand Christian Reconstruction. This is what we are talking about in every area of life: being subjected to futility, and then being released and obtaining the freedom and the glory of the children of God. That's what it's all about!

So are we thinking big enough? In Rushdoony's essay, we learned about how Marxism has an agenda. Do you think Christianity has an agenda? Does Jesus have an agenda? Is He trying to do something? Yes! Are we tied into that agenda? Do we understand what it is? If you don't think Christianity has an agenda– just re-read the Great Commission and find out if we're supposed to be active. Think about that!

Business is an Exchange of Value

As far as business is concerned, business is engaged in the marketplace, and the market is where there is an exchange of value between two free agents. For instance, you have a doohickey, I have money. A doohickey is worth this much money; that's how much you're selling it for. You say, "I want money. So we'll make an exchange." We agree. Boom! Business. That's all it is. It's an exchange of value. I see the value in the doohickey, you see the value in the money.

At my house, we once had a cute, fuzzy cat we got for free. She wasn't fixed, so we ended up with a litter of super cute kittens. I told my wife, "Let's sell the kittens."
She said, "Great! How much do kittens go for?"
"I have no idea. It depends on the value that someone sees in it." Exchange of value is what I'm thinking.

I told my wife, "Let's sell them for a hundred bucks."
She told me, "You're crazy. Nobody's going to buy a kitten for a hundred bucks!"

"Well, what if you take the perfect pictures of them. You know? Do your photography thing. We'll post those online and let people decide."

She took the pictures, and I put them up on Facebook. Big mistake! I suggest you don't ever do that. On Facebook, you get all the naysayers and trolls publicly telling you that they think you're an idiot. I don't want to see that.

Honestly, I don't care what they think. So we took the listing off of facebook. I decided instead to list the kittens on Craigslist. My thinking was, "If you like it, contact me. If you don't like it, I don't care."

What happened? Boom! Phone call. Phone call. Phone call...

"Can I have a kitten?" "Can I have a kitten?" "Can I have a kitten?"

"Save it for me, I'll send you money, PayPal, whatever."

My wife is wondering, "What happened?"

I said, "Value! I showed value in a kitten!" Right? The people on Facebook are saying, "Oh, you can get a kitten for $20. What you're doing is wrong, blah blah blah."

I responded, "Great, go get your $20 kitten elsewhere. This one's $100!"

I'm convinced that the more investment you make in something, the more you value it. If you paid for a book, you did so because you are getting value out of it. If you got it for free, it wouldn't mean as much to you. Likewise, if I gave someone a kitten for free, they might abuse the kitten, and I don't want that to happen. But if they invest a little bit more in it, they're going to take care of that kitten.

Eventually, we had another litter of kittens, and we sold those kittens for $100. It kept going.

One of the beauties of the realities of each family being given a diversification of God-given talents is that we can individually impact our culture, and specifically, the marketplace according to our particular giftings.

Just because your friends are working in a thriving firearms business doesn't mean you have to be engaged in that field. Nor does the fact that your friends are all selling essential oils mean that you also have to get into that particular market. There is a wide variety of services that society needs, and we each can be engaged in the specific veins that are important to us.

A Business That Shapes Culture

Do you think that the marketplace can move culture? Have you heard of the new Amazon headquarters? Is the search for its new location moving the culture? Yes, it is! There are cities all over this country that are saying, "Amazon, please, will you come here? We have these beautiful bridges and water. We have tax breaks. Please, please, please come here!" Amazon has a super powerful business model, and they know they're going to employ a lot of people, so the business is shaping the culture in these cities because the company is very, very strong.

Again, do you think that the market place is impacting the culture? Do most people know about Uber? It was started in 2008 with no app and no cars. By 2014 it had grown from zero dollars to three billion dollars in worth. In six years! The app didn't even come out until halfway through that time.

I don't know if you're a Trump fan or not, and I don't put any faith in Trump, but there's one thing he's succeeded in doing, and that is increasing jobs. I have a friend who is the commanding officer of the recruiting district in Philadelphia, and he just had to go to the Admiral recently because recruiting is down. Why is recruiting down? Because the marketplace is up and jobs are available! People can get work, and people don't want to join the military when jobs are readily available.

When jobs are scarce, a military job equals security. The military is safe because they're going to get paid regularly. Sure, they may have to do drudgerous tasks (trust me, I'm in the military), but at least they will get paid. There's a schedule they can see, and they can understand how it works. It all makes sense, while the marketplace is amorphous, and we don't know what could happen. There's a constant fear of losing my job, but at least people now see that there's an opportunity, and they believe that they can make it work.

If Trump gets re-elected, that's six more years of the kind of marketplace that we're experiencing now. What was Uber able to achieve in six years? Do you think something similar is still possible? I would say it's even *doubly* possible now because they did that four years ago! In public schools, today students are told that if they apply certain rules, there can be an expected outcome. Why? Because we know about truth, that God is covenantal, and that truth exists. But students of business realize they need to understand the same principles as systems, the keys to the marketplace. If you want to build a strong business, build a robust but simple system.

Find a Need

The marketplace is about finding a need in your community and providing a superior service that delivers that need. The wise entrepreneur will see needs that others don't, and make an investment of time, money, and energy that will deliver that need. For families to build strong businesses, it is necessary to be engaged and involved with the society around you.

Needs can arise locally or nationally, and whichever direction your business will take, remember that by providing a superior service you will be able to build a strong and valuable business.

Recommended Book List

There is so much that we can learn about building a business that lasts. I'll recommend for you a few of the resources that I have found beneficial:

Rich Dad, Poor Dad by Robert Kiyosaki—You need to get this book and read it! In it, the author says things like, "The poor and the middle-class work for money, and the rich and wealthy have money working for them," because money is a tool, a resource. Are you thinking, "I need to do this because I need to make money"? Or are you thinking, "I need to do something, and I want to use money as a tool to make my vision happen." There's a big difference!

Winning the Battle for the Minds of Men by Dennis Peacocke—Is an excellent book, especially for young men.

Families in Covenant Succession by Jason Diffner -Another excellent and practical book. The author talks about having a big vision for your family, and how to execute it. It addresses how you should be thinking about what your family is going to be doing in the future, and how to take practical steps to think in that manner.

Building an Empire by Brian Carruthers—This is an inspiring book about building a massive empire in the industry of network marketing. Very practical with easy to follow steps to build a big network, which is extremely important in any business industry, especially network marketing.

Faith on Earth by Lou Poumakis—If you don't know much about Christian Reconstruction, this book explains it very simply. It's an excellent book to get started.

Do you know how to make a better hamburger than McDonald's? Of course you do! But how many of you can build a better system than McDonald's? McDonald's is successful because every time you see those golden arches, you think, "Fries and a Big Mac!" They've created a system that they can replicate over and over again, and distribute it across the entire world. The systems are important. *The E-Myth Revisited* discusses the value of systems.

The Millionaire Real Estate Investor by Gary Keller—This is helpful if you're interested in real estate. I found this at a garage sale and bought it for a quarter, but it's worth far more than that investment! You can find these books in the library.

The Biblical Trustee Family by Andrea Schwartz—This is a great book to help you understand how family relationships work. Do you have a trustee relationship? Are you collecting assets for a multigenerational purpose? Are you cultivating them right now and passing them onto the next generation? You need to be teaching the next generation to be responsible for those assets.

Building Wealth One House At A Time by John Schwab—A fantastic book on real estate. Schwab talks about making your way in real estate slowly. If you understand how the real estate industry works, you don't have to have massive amounts of cash flow to get it to go.

The Business of the 21st Century by Robert Kiyosaki
Could you make it to a far away destination by walking? You could. You could walk or even crawl if you wanted. Would it take you a while? Sure! Could you have gotten here in a Growler jet? Yes. The vehicle you choose can get you to your destination faster than others, but it's still just a vehicle. This book talks about that principle.

Economics in One Lesson by Henry Haslet
This is a book you need to get if you don't understand economics. It breaks down how people try to corrupt you, and use faulty logic to try to make you understand how economics functions.

Doing Business God's Way by Dennis Peacocke
This is really fundamental, and will help you understand economics, increase, property, and service. In the business field, you want to take care of your customers. You want them to be happy and comfortable and have their needs met. You want to give them premium service. To have a fantastic business, you will do really well by serving others.

A business model that makes other people successful is a recipe for success. The Bible says, "He who makes himself first will be last." But he who puts himself last will be first! That's a service mentality. "How can I take care of other people through whatever resources I have at my disposal?" If you take care of them, money and wealth are just a byproduct of how that exchange of value is occurring.

The Myth of the Rich Doctor by Vicki Rackner
This is helpful if you're interested in the medical field and want to know how doctors are working. It's all about mentality, and how people view money and their businesses. If you help people unlock how they think about their business, it can expand their business and potential.

God wants to inspire us. We are tools in His hands, and the better and sharper we are, the more useful we are to Him. A dull knife is not very useful, but one that's razor-sharp, He can use us with precision in what He's executing. I pray you all become excellent tools in the Lord's hands.

Reintegrating Family in Family Business

By Dan Stachofsky

There's a significant question I'd like for us to consider. How do we integrate the family into a family business in a way that honors God and furthers the multigenerational visions that we are learning about and being challenged and inspired for?

As we consider the answer to this, let me start with a story about a boy who grew up in the 1930s who said, "There's got to be a better way to do retail." In high school, he was voted "the most versatile." He was someone who thought outside the box. "How do we do this differently? How can we be more efficient and effective in what we're trying to do?"

He got a job at J.C. Penney and then went to the war where he did intelligence. When he came back, he said, "I want to get into business on my own."

His dad was a banker who said, "I'm going to invest twenty-five thousand dollars in you." His dad saw this boy's potential and said, "I'm a banker. You're not going into banking, but I'm going to invest in you anyway," and gave him twenty-five thousand dollars.

He bought a Ben Franklin franchise and went on to build about four of those. Then he asked, "Since these are only in the city, why don't we put some in rural areas?" But the Ben

Franklins said, "No we don't want to do that," so he went out on his own. He turned $25,000 into one hundred and thirty billion! He had an idea, and his father invested in him.

Do you know what brand I'm talking about? Walmart! That's right. So now the family is worth over a hundred and thirty-five billion. Walmart itself is worth more than that, but the family is the wealthiest family in the world, all because a father decided to believe in and invest in his son.

I didn't have time to do the math and see what the value of $25,000 would have been in the 40s, but he wasn't just saying, "Here's a thousand; let's see what you can do. Try making a lemonade stand." It was probably like a hundred thousand, or something. His father was saying, "I'm investing in you, and we're going to invest in the family."

Sam Walton began Walmart with his brother. It started with the family, and the family still owns it. It's a publicly traded company, but the family is still highly involved as the leadership and management of the company, and most of them have faith. They aren't loud about philanthropy, but this next generation is coming in– similarly to the Rockefellers—saying, "We can do more!" Their long-range goal is to make known how much they're going to give for philanthropy, and this year it's about four hundred and forty-five million a year!

They started with only twenty-five thousand dollars and a father who said, "I'm going to invest in my son. It might not be exactly what I would be doing, but we'll start a family business." And look at what he did for the family! Hopefully, that inspires you.

Now I'm going to take a step back and look at some of the oldest family businesses today. In some ways, any private business is a family business. It has the social security number of the guy who founded it. Most of us work in a private business of some sort, so we're building somebody's family economy.

Here are some industries that are some of the world's oldest family-run businesses: construction, hospitality, paper, wine, goldsmith, shipbuilding, a lot of standard, staple industries.

The oldest family business we know of is going into its 40th generation. It was founded in the year 578. How old is that, about 1440 years old? But they didn't really have a choice in starting it. It's a Japanese company, and the emperor at the time took this family out of Korea and said, "You're going to build me a really nice Buddhist temple." And they did it. They aren't believers. They aren't building the Kingdom of God, but they've established something that their family has been doing for 1,400 years.

They could have done it begrudgingly, but they said, "We're going to do an excellent job where we are, with what we're given." 1400 years later, they're still in construction in Japan. This family still builds amazing temples and other buildings, and they're well known. If you want to build something that will be remembered for years to come, you should talk to this family!

There is another building that has become the oldest family hotel in the world. It's celebrating it's 1,300th anniversary this year. It was founded in 718. Hōshi Ryokan is in Japan. This family found a hot spring, and build a hotel on the site. Next to it, and for the next thirteen hundred years, this family has been practicing hospitality.

In another instance, there's a family winery; the oldest family winery in history. It's in France and was founded in the year 1000. The pictures of this place are absolutely amazing! It's a true chateau. It looks like a castle with amazing gardens. This family has been making wine for a thousand years.

And then you've got the oldest family business in America. It was started in Italy. It's the Avedis Zildjian Company, the cymbal company. They moved to Massachusetts, but they founded the company in 1623, and they've been making cymbals ever since then.

The oldest family farm in America is the Tuttle farm in Dover, N.H, founded in 1635. The founder, John Tuttle, left England, survived a shipwreck off the Maine coast, and arrived in Dover with his wife and four-year-old daughter. They had a vision as a family.

A very successful family-owned company is S.C. Johnson. They're a publicly owned company, but they let it be known that they are a family business. Yes, there's marketing in that because they're selling products your family is going to use, but the family is still involved. They found a way to continue operating as a family business, and yet their vision was bigger than that. It was bigger than just the nuclear family.

Instead of asking, "What are my kids going to do with me?" they realized that "Maybe we don't have the best finance person in our family. Okay, we're going to hire somebody to do that for us. We're going to build out the team that's going to make us successful, but it's going to run with the family in mind."

I believe that any company that we can own, any entrepreneur that owns a business, is building a family economy. The family economy is what's going to be recapitalized so that we can invest in the next generation.

When we think of it that way, it gives us a vision that says, "Everyone that we bring into this business is part of this vision. They're part of the family, and we're going to treat them like family. We don't need unions in our businesses because we're going to be treating people like our family."

A family business is the most durable wealth-creating vehicle available today because you're recapitalizing! The book *Family Wealth* talks about not just financial wealth, but about the knowledge and skills that generate wealth and take your wealth into the local community and the culture at large. By reinvesting in your family, you're putting that money back where it belongs and keeping it there.

Rushdoony says, "The family is the basic economic unit of society. No society can prosper which weakens the family, either by removing its responsibilities for education and welfare, or by limiting the families of control of its properties and inheritance by usurpation."

Families must also be sure not to *limit* their family's influence. We've probably all heard the stories about the industrial revolution. There was a time when families worked as a family unit, and they would build their business and pass it down to the next generation. The cobbler was a cobbler's family for generations. We just looked at families who were in hospitality for thirteen hundred years! But with the industrial revolution, the fathers and mothers were taken out of the home. The kids were sent to school. As a result, the family got weakened. And now we're reaping the fruit today.

What we're calling you back to in this symposium is to strengthen the family by having a vision that's bigger than ourselves, and that's going to strengthen what's been weakened.

As a father, you might not be the most visionary one in the family. Maybe your wife is, or perhaps some of your children are. Tap into that! It's okay. God has blessed us with a family that is diverse, talented, and skilled, and we get to tap into what it is that we're building. We want to create a legacy.

In Proverbs 5 there is the story of a woman who was living in sin. She does not ponder the path of life. Her ways wander. And here's the thing: she does not know it! She is outside the covering of her family. She's on her own. How many of us have been there? How many of us have willingly left the covering of our family to go off on our own and wander? And we don't even know it!

But here's the flip side: *"God, you make known to me the path of life, and in Your presence is the fullness of joy."* We're looking for joy. We're looking for pleasures in our family, society, church, everywhere. We're looking for that joy, and sometimes we go off in our own, thinking that we'll find out own way. But what the Psalmist is saying is, no! God, *You* make known to me the path of life, in *Your* presence is the fullness of joy, and at *Your* right hand are pleasures forevermore. So we don't need to wander. We need to go to God and ask, "What is the path of life?"

Jesus was asked by a lawyer, "What is the greatest law?" In response, essentially He said, "Well, it's about relationship." Isn't that what these commandments are about? *"Thou shalt love the Lord thy God will all thy heart, soul, and mind, and you shall love thy neighbor as thyself."*

It's not about the law, it's about relationships. Isn't the family about relationship? Yes, there are times when we're training in discipline and discipleship, but if we're going to be in a family business, we have also got to find a way to be in relationship with our children and spouses. If we're not loving our neighbor and family as ourselves, the family is going to leave us. The title of this talk is "reintegrating the family into the family business." If we don't know how to love the members of our family as we love ourselves, it very well may be that they go off on their own and find different paths.

164

Sam Walton's dad said, "Hey, you're not going to be a banker like me, but I'm still going to invest in you."

Rockefeller did that too, right? They saw that it still needed to be part of what they're doing. We need to recast our vision, fathers, and realize, "Okay, I thought we were going to be a banking family, but now we're going to be a banking and retail family. Or maybe we're going to be a banking, retail, and online business family. Let's expand it and let it grow with the family that God has given us! He's given us a very unique family with special talents."

Building a lasting family business is all about loving your neighbor as yourself. It is about loving your children, loving your family as yourself. How do we do that? By building a lasting family, and I think there are five ways to do that:

1. Know your purpose—This idea has come up a couple times this weekend already. Matthew 23:11 says, "Whoever is greatest among you shall be your servant." and Malachi 4:6 says, "And he shall turn the hearts of the fathers to their children and the children to their fathers, lest I strike the land with utter destruction."

So, know what our purpose is! This can be hard to find out, but there is a process known as finding your core principle statement. What is the core statement, the core principle that your family stands for? "We're going to influence the culture this way." Maybe your family is about hospitality. Maybe your family is about ministry to orphans, and all the businesses are going to revolve around that as the core theme. What is the core principle that your family is going to stand for? What is your purpose?

Your purpose is to serve, as fathers and mothers, our children, and to build them up. Sam Walton's dad served him. He wasn't coerced into the banking industry. He basically said, "I'm going to serve you by giving you these talents."

Think of the parable of the talents. The master gave one servant ten talents, and he trusted him. Because he entrusted him with it, the servant went and got ten more. The servant with five talents got five more. They took the responsibility of that and carried the weight of it, and it built character. They had the character to say, "This is a responsibility, and I'm going to build on it."

Do your children know your core principle? If they were asked in church on Sunday what your family's core principle is, could they answer? If not, then talk to them, and build it. If you have older kids, build it together. Bring them into it. Ask them, "What should our family be about? We can all assess each others' talents and skills. We want to build a family that's going to be around for four hundred years."

Bring them into the discussion. Ask for their opinion. That draws them into the relationship and makes them part of it. In management, you learn that if you want to win over your employees with the direction of your business or the objective you're setting, you need to make them part of that objective. If you do, then they have ownership, they have skin in the game, and then they're going to perform. They'll say, "Okay, how do I take that and turn it into gold?" Children want to be a part of that too. They want to be a part of the big plan.

2. Write down your vision or plan and review it regularly —Begin with the history. What brought you to this point? Become a great communicator! Challenge yourself. It might be rough to begin with, but challenge yourself to be a great communicator. Start telling stories. Tell a story about your grandparents, your family. Tell allegories about where you want the future to go. Start casting a big vision. Help them dream. They want to be part of something bigger than themselves.

3. Then speak to the present—"Where are we right now as a family?" **Assess your skills, talents, and interests**. It may be that you've spent most of your career building up a family business that your kids don't want to be a part of, and that can be hard.

I don't think that being part of the family business needs to be binary. Say you're in hospitality and they don't want to be part of the bed and breakfast you've built up over this many years. That doesn't mean they're not part of the family business. I don't think it's binary like that. We have to think about the in-between. What's a creative solution for that? What do the kids want to be a part of? How can that be molded into that vision? How can your vision be changed to include what your kids are interested in? Draw them into it.

If you're asking their opinions, speaking the history, speaking to the vision of the future, I believe they're going to be interested. It might be just on the holidays, or you might have them over for lunch when they ask you, "How's your business doing?" That's them being part of your family business! Maybe that's just where you're at right now. But they're showing curiosity, they're showing interest. That's part of them being part of the family business.

There's a coffee shop in Spokane. The dad became an apprentice to a coffee maker who'd been in the industry 52 years. He'd been all over, and actually helped start up Seattle's Best coffee. He had a coffee shop in the Anacortes area, and now he's in Spokane where he started rebuilding a coffee shop. But he's getting older, and he needed someone else to start taking over, so he tapped his banker, a guy he'd worked with to get his business loans and everything he needed to get started. The banker was a family man, and he saw in this man a vision.

Well, the banker started learning about the coffee, and it was in a true apprenticeship model. Chris is his name, and he didn't know anything about coffee except that he liked to drink it, and he could tell the difference between good and bad coffee. He started sitting under the teaching of this guy, Gary, and Gary taught him everything he knew. He taught him how to roast, where to source the beans from. Meanwhile, Chris had a son who was graduating high school, and his parents had been pressuring him, "Hey, where are you going to go to college? Because when you graduate, we want to tell everyone."

Well, Chris didn't want to do that. He wanted to learn a trade. But he didn't want to learn the coffee trade, and his dad was kind of bummed about that. Instead, Chris went into construction and a couple other things, and about seven years later, his dad said, "Hey, Chris, we have an opening." And finally, his son was ready and wanted to come do that. So now he's in the coffee business, and he's learning. His dad said, "If I hadn't let him go, he would never have had the chance to learn so many of the things that he brings to the business today that he learned from other people."

So it might be that your children need to learn certain things from other businesses before they're ready to invest in your family business. Let's not be afraid, or binary in our vision for our kids. I think the apprenticeship model is great, and we can learn a lot from it.

4. We need to have counsel outside the nuclear family—
If you want a long term family business, you have to build a solid foundation for success. Proverbs 11:14 says that

where there is no guidance the people fall, but in an abundance of counselors there is safety.

Get outside the family when you're thinking about structuring your business. There are a lot of things to consider, and you have to build a team. Legal. Financial. Those are two critical things that, if you don't have them nailed down or have a good partner, can really thwart your efforts a multi-generational family business.

a. Marketing—Marketing is one of the things that sounds so easy, but in reality, it is so hard. If you know a good person who understand marketing, pay them what they're worth. Pay them on the results of their marketing campaigns. Pay them generously, because it will be the difference between your business floundering or being hugely successful.

At one time, Apple was struggling and was about to go out of business. Steve Jobs had left, and their marketing was terrible. They were introducing the iMac, and they were planning a whole ad in the New York Times about all the achievements this computer could do. But the ad was LONG. It was like reading a block of words. Consequently, their sales were terrible. It was the worst ad in history!

But then Steve Jobs came back, and meanwhile, he had purchased DreamWorks, a movie company all about story. He said, "The hero is the customer. All that long block of text did was talk about how great our computer was, but it didn't talk about how great the customer would be with our computer."

So they started the iPod by saying, "Listen to great music anywhere!" They designed the advertisements with a geeky PC guy and a really hip Apple guy. It had nothing to do with the product, but it was branding, marketing, and by it, they became the #1 tech company until this year when Microsoft took them back. It's all about marketing!

b. Mastermind Groups — The other aspect of seeking counsel outside your a family is this concept that I found in Isaiah 41. This is a big topic right now in the online business world, called mastermind groups. Some people spend $500 a month, some spend $10,000 a month to be in mastermind groups, to be part of these groups with other experts who are doing similar things. They meet for an hour a week, and one person is on the hot seat. They can ask about any business problem, opportunity, or project, and they can get feedback from these other experts.

$10,000 a month seems like a lot to spend unless you have a multimillion dollar business. To get that kind of counsel and feedback is amazing. Well, I'd been hearing about it in the business world, but then I came across it in Isaiah 41:6. And how amazing is it that God had this in His plans way back when?

"Everyone helps his neighbor and says to his brother 'be strong.'"

That's edification! That's encouragement! And it's not referring just to your spiritual state, because in the next verse, Isaiah 41:7 says, *"The craftsman strengthens the goldsmith, and he who smooths with the hammer, him who strikes the anvil says to the soldering, 'it is good," and they strengthen it with nails so it cannot be moved."*

Here are people in different businesses, encouraging one another. The craftsman strengthens the goldsmith. He's working in jewelry or something, and he's struggling. "I don't know how to make this piece of gold do it what I want it to do." Then the craftsman strengthens him, encourages him, helps him.

How many people are in your life who own businesses and are encouraging and inspiring you as a leader? Do you have people you can go to and safely say, "I don't know yet if this is the right direction. I need counsel, I need help from people who are like minded."

Maybe there are people in this room that you can say, "We need to start meeting together. We need to make our own mastermind group." You're going to be encouraging one another in building the kingdom of God according to principles found in God's word, which is what we need today to strengthen the family and build a multigenerational business. These mastermind groups can be super powerful. They can transform the business.

Counsel outside the family isn't just about professional services; it's also finding neighbors who say to their brothers, "Be strong! Your business is going through a difficult time, but be strong. Have faith. Trust God. He's going to see you through it. Let's talk brass tacks about your business."

Maybe your marketing isn't great. Maybe your product needs to be shifted. What was good ten years ago isn't good now, so perhaps you need to do a little more with your product.

I really encourage you guys to think about becoming part of mastermind groups. Seek them out. They're really good if they're 5 or 6 people, but you can also do them online via Zoom or whatever.

5) Prepare your children—Include them early. For those of you whose children aren't fully grown yet, include them early on.

I've got a couple of businesses that I've been trying to get off the ground, and I talk about them at home. I talk about them with my wife. I talk about them around the dinner table, and the kids hear about them. They know what we're doing.

We were down in the Grand Canyon a couple months ago, and as we were going through the gift shop, my nine-year-old daughter saw a vest that was just perfect for a project that we have. She said, "Dad! Dad! I found exactly what we're looking for!" I didn't tell her to do that, but she got excited to realize she could help me with something I was struggling with, something I was looking for. She's involved! It's amazing, and it's so perfect.

Yesterday we were in Leavenworth, and I was working on these talks in our hotel room while my family went down and started lunch. I get a call from my wife who said, "You need to bring your business cards and some information here because our waitress wants to become a distributor for us."

It was my seven-year-old daughter who had sold this waitress on the fantastic quality of our product and how she should help me with the business!

I thought, "Okay, I thought this was going to happen in maybe 5-10 years from now!" But we're including our children early, and they know about what we're doing. We get in the habit of asking their opinion, and it draws them in.

Again, it's about relationships. If we are only about the tasks of building the business and of selling the product, then we're missing the relationship. We have to slow down! When I'm in business at my office, I don't like to chit chat a whole lot. It's probably one of my biggest weakness. But for the last ten years, I've been in relationship selling, and when I'm with my customers, I slow down and talk to them about everything. When I'm back in an office setting, I just want to get work done.

If we're like that with our family or anyone who's a part of our business, we're going to drive them away really fast. People that we've hired who aren't part of our nuclear family want to be part of a family business because they don't want to be only about the money. They want it to be more relational. Yes, there are goals, and yes, you have to manage your people. But you have to slow down and bring them in, and be about relationship! Again, love your neighbor as yourself.

It's okay to let them fail. Actually, you only learn through your failures. If you're only ever succeeding, you're going to become very prideful. It's from failure that we grow and that we succeed. Probably one of the hardest things to do as your kids get older is to let them fail; to know that the decision that they're making right now is actually a bad decision. But if you let them go through that process, they're going to come out understanding that it was a bad one, and they're going to learn from it. You get to disciple and train through the failures, and they'll be more valuable to the business.

There's a fundamental leadership principle we need to consider: Any CEO who's going to be successful has learned the importance of pursuing excellence, not perfection. Unfortunately, we aspire to perfection in our kids sometimes. We expect them to obey the first time. We expect them to do the dishes right after dinner. We expect perfection. But in the business context, as your kids grow up and become part of the business, pursuing perfection is the #1 way to get nothing done and to drive your family and others away.

They won't like working for you if you expect perfection. But if you're pursuing excellence, then you're letting them go beyond your own understanding. You might say, "Hey, I want a website build," and your vision of a website might be basic. But you'll find out that they will put their whole weight behind it because they're pursuing excellence. Instead of limiting themselves to what your definition of excellence is, they're actually becoming creative and going far beyond your understanding of what the ideal website would have been.

So, pursue excellence! Encourage your family and employees to pursue excellence, and have excellence as an active, agile part of your culture. It will help ensure that your legacy is secure throughout the ages, I believe.
Gortex has over 300 products. You'd think that in a business, it's not good to proliferate your product line. It's difficult to manage and build like that. But Gortex created a culture that says, "If you have a good idea, we'll allow 20% or so of your time to go after that idea, and we'll invest in that idea, we'll see it through, and we'll measure progress.

You get to rally your own team around that product if you have an idea. You get to solicit other people's help, and say, 'Hey, I know what you're working on right now, but if I could have just 10% of your time over the next 4 weeks, here's my pitch. Here's the product I'm working on.'"

That's how Gortex was pitched. That's how the actual product was developed. They do a lot more than just the covering over the coats now, but they practice the culture that says employees pursue excellence, and we reward that and invest in you. So let's do that! Let's invest in our businesses.

Now here are a couple warnings and cautions.

We are at war, and the enemy is real. So we need to be on our guard. "Behold I set an angel before you to guard you on the way and to bring you to the place that I have prepared," says Exodus 23:20. Luke 12:15 says, "And he said to them 'take care. Be on your guard against all covetousness. For one's life does not consist in the abundance of his possessions.

There is more to this life than building a billion-dollar business. How you go about building your family business is more important than the end result. The harvest is up to the Lord. We are about watering and planting. We need to be considering our ways, and being on board.

To the children who are part of a family whose dad is casting a vision, I want to really encourage you to assess yourself. Are you potentially thwarting your father's vision and the work that he is aspiring? Daughters, are you being the woman in Proverbs 5 who's left the covering of her house and is living in sin? Don't wander! Appreciate the value of your home and the house your parents are building. Appreciate the church you're part of. The elders that are there have your best interest in mind. Don't wander! It never pays off. It leads to death. We are on a path of life. Surrender your own covetousness, and let God guide you in the way of life. Look to your father and mother, who know you, for wisdom and advice on how best to pursue business.

Here are some practical steps:

Include your children in business meetings. They get to be a part of it, prepare for it. They learn from you how to be in a meeting, how to be about business, and how to organize the right deal with that customer. That's discipleship and apprenticeship. That's walking along talking along with them.

Join a mastermind group, or something similar. You need counsel from friends who are committed to your success and want you to be super successful. So don't be alone.

I can't speak too much to this, but I know it's essential: Prepare to pass it on. At the end, if you die, know what will happen with your business. Jason Diffner's book *Covenant Family Succession* is beneficial here. *Family Wealth* is very helpful here. Have that covenant, that trust. Work on building those. They take work. Maybe one of your children is better at organizing that than you are. Delegate that. It's better and very helpful.

Have a 200+ year plan. Cast a vision that's way bigger than yourself. And as your family is developing this, you may have to employ four quadrant planning. Start doing what you need to do to capitalize that vision. Know what you need to *stop* doing. There are some things you're doing now that you need to stop because they're not moving you forward. Stop those things and start other things. Some things you need to do more of, some less of.

A very practical idea is to quickly assess where you need to be spending your time.

I'll close with a quote from Ken Blanchard, the author of *The One Minute Manager*, an excellent book on how to manage people. I think as families, as we transition our children into adulthood and partnership, these are sound principles.

> *"The best minutes I spend are the ones I spend investing in people. What was Jesus's ministry all about with his 12 disciples? He invested in them daily. He walked with them daily. He invested in people. It's all about loving others more than yourself."*

Blanchard recommends setting three goals for everyone involved in your business which you can review in one minute or less. Now, I have younger kids. When I consider what they've done in a day, it takes more than one minute. I need to get better at that.

But use one minute praise to give your employees and family positive feedback. It just takes one minute. Catch them doing something great. Then, take one minute to reprimand them. "You know what you just did? Let's change that." In just one minute, say what it was. Don't belabor it. And then give them a picture of how to do it right, and empower them to do it. Hold them accountable, and then do a one minute review. It doesn't take long to review.

Celebrate often. You want your family to be excited to be in business with you. Celebrate any reason to celebrate. Have fun doing family business. It's going to take intentionality. It can take a long time. Days turned to weeks, weeks turn to months before you realize, "Wow! We've been working hard, and we haven't taken time to celebrate or recognize that people are doing a great job."

If they're putting excellence in, celebrate it! Catch them doing the right thing and encourage them. Make them want to do it better. Say their names– that induces dopamine in their brain that says, "Ooh, I like that!" Tell them one thing they were doing really well. They're going to want to do it again and again for you.

I think this is a good foundation. There's a lot more that could be said, but I think the big thing is to be intentional. Set a big vision for our families. Get it to be bigger than ourselves. How is this business going to become bigger than ourselves? People want to be involved in big things. Make it bigger! Cast a vision! Maybe this could be a good set of tools for you.

Hospitality is a big growing industry. There's always a demand for it. When people stay in your hotel or B&B, you have so many opportunities to bless them by making it clean and comfortable. You get to invest in them, and there are so many ways your kids can be a part of that, with so many skills. If you have a house or B&B, no matter what your skill set is, your family can be involved.

The online marketplace is growing. We don't realize how much knowledge and information we each have. We may have years of experience in a career that we could turn into an online business where we're coaching other people to do what you're doing.

How do you scale yourself and replicate what you're doing? Your daily routine may be second nature to you, but not to other people. You can set a pattern for them, and give them workshops that they can learn from online. You may have skills that you've been using in working for someone else that you could employ online and have people pay you for that information.

There are also a lot of trades like real estate you can do as a family. My family sells products that help balance your nervous and immune systems through vibration and frequencies. They're very portable, something you can wear. For functional medicine or holistic doctors, it can really benefit their therapies for their patients. It helps in recovering from stress and injuries and creates an environment where your body can be treated and heal more effectively.

There is a multitude of ideas and businesses that your family can plug into!

Thank you all very much. I enjoyed the process of putting this talk together. Thank you all.

Crown of Thorns

By Rev. Michael Kloss

This sermon came out of a series of sermons, so I have to explain something that I'm presupposing here before I begin. If you have Bibles, turn with me to the beginning of Genesis chapter two. If we don't get this right at the very start, everything else I'm going to say is not going to make any sense.

Genesis 2:5 says something very interesting:

> *Now no shrub of the field had yet grown on the earth,*
> *and no plant of the field had yet sprouted, for the*
> *Lord God had not caused it to rain on the earth, and*
> *there was no man to cultivate the ground.*

Now, what I find fascinating here is that there was no man to work the ground– as if that was the chief end of man here, at this point. God doesn't say that, "There was not yet man to worship Me." He doesn't say, "There's not yet man to build the temple." He says, "There's not a man to work." God created a world, and He put man in it because He had a plan. His plan required him to create man.

Truthfully, I think most of us believe that work is the result of the Fall. We fell, Adam was naked and happy with his wife in the garden eating fruit all day long, and that was Paradise. If we could just get back to Paradise! Remember that old blues song, "In heaven you never have to change your socks, the whisky flows off the rocks, and handouts grow on trees." That's an old blues song, but I think most of us think that's what heaven is like– especially the part about the whiskey.

But Genesis 2:15 is *pre*-Fall:

> *"The Lord God took the man and placed him in the orchard in Eden to work it and to keep it."*

Now, the ESV says "keep it," but it should be "guard it," which leads to all kinds of questions. Before the Fall, what was Adam told to guard it from? Why is God telling Adam to guard it when everything was very good? Well, that's a sermon for another day.

God told Adam to work it, and He put him in the Garden because He wanted him to till it. He wanted man to protect it. How does he protect it? By obeying the Law of God. In this presentation, this is where we're starting. Everything I'm going to say presupposes this: Man was made to work.

We thought man was made to worship. Yes– but work is worship. You don't go out into the world during the week, and then go to worship on Sunday. You go into the world *and* you worship God all week long with your work as an individual and as a family, and then you gather on Sunday to worship Him corporately. It's *all* worship.

This is the intent of God from the beginning. So if we're reconstructing something, *this* is what we're reconstructing. We're reconstructing— faithful obedience to the Word of God so we can go into the world to work and keep it.

We all know what happened next. Adam and Eve were in the garden, but it didn't stay happy and fun. Romans 8:19-21:

For the creation waits in eager expectation for the children of God to be revealed. For the creation was subjected to futility, not by its own choice, but by the will of the one who subjected it, in hope that the creation itself will be liberated from its bondage to decay and obtain the freedom of the glory of the children of God.

"Obtain the freedom of the glory of the children of God." God, who commanded us to be fruitful, to subdue, and to multiply in order to fill the earth, issued a judgment that makes fruitfulness far more difficult. Childbirth is more painful. Adam, who failed to obey God is now estranged from the two necessary ingredients to fruitfulness. This is the curse.

God doesn't say, "Now I don't want you to be fruitful." That command is still there, but the curse is that now the command is far more difficult. The two things that Adam needed if he was going to be fruitful are his wife, and the ground.

But Adam's helpmate now suffers more in childbirth, and the ground yields more than fruit– it yields thorns. Thorns come up out of the ground now to frustrate man's work.

Having been commissioned to fruitfulness through childbirth and subduing the world, man and woman fell into sin, and therefore pain was added to what God created them to do. Thorns now exist where once the ground yielded willingly.

I was trimming the hedges in my yard once on a beautiful summer day. We have rented this house for 10 years, and there were people renting it for 10 years before that. It is like the garden of Eden! If you ever want to know what the Garden of Eden was like, my yard is like that. So I was out there happily trimming the hedge while beautiful dragonflies and birds flew around the yard.

I have an electric trimmer that doesn't have much horsepower, but despite that, I was just trimming along, praising God over how magnificent this was. But on the other side of the bush– on my neighbor's side– was a huge blackberry stem, almost as big as my arm. (Every time I tell this story, it gets even bigger.) The trimmer was strong enough to bend it, but not break it– and that thing came whipping across the top and literally stuck in my face! I thought, "This is like the Fall! Here I am in paradise, and now I've got thorns sticking out of my face!" Of course, you could hear the kids on the other end of the yard just howling because there I was having to pull the thing out of my face.

I think this is what we all experience. You're going along on your merry way thinking, "This is how God intended the world to be"…when suddenly you get whipped in the face by a bunch of thorns!

Thorns attack us, they attack our fruitfulness, they attack our joy, they attack our faith.

Now Eve was told that her desire would be for her husband. The term rendered "desire" occurs only three times in the Old Testament, the other two times being in Genesis 4:7 and Song of Solomon 7:10.

Now let's look at Genesis 4:7. God tells Cain that his "desire" is contrary to him, and sin's desire is to rule over him. *"Sin waits at the door and its desire is to rule over you."* This is the same word that is applied to Eve in Genesis 3:16. Sin wants to determine his actions. Sin wants him to follow *it*– not the other way around.

The use of this word "desire" in both cases suggests that Eve's desire for her husband is a desire to determine his actions, and the man's rule over the woman will be a rejection and suppression of her influence. Right? She's a helpmate! But what will happen now is that he's not going to want to listen to her. These two realities– the man as a project and the man who doesn't listen– are realities that I believe are in *all* of our lives. How often does that joke come up, right? "He doesn't listen!" Wives, can I get an 'amen' here? Right? He doesn't!

I work at a court where a couple came to get a marriage license. That isn't what we do, and she had told him it was the wrong place. As they were asking me questions, I told them this was the wrong place, and he said to her, "I should have listened to you." I said, "Welcome to marriage!" He said, "Oh, because she's always right?" I said, "No, because even when she *is* right, you never want to listen to her. This is what marriage is like!"

Thorns come up, and we all know how difficult fruitfulness is. Look at all these marriages, and when all these kids come along, how much *more* difficult is it now? We don't want to listen to our wives, and they want to rule over us!

We have six kids, but everyone teases my wife that she has seven. The problem is, I largely make that statement true by the way that I act sometimes. But my wife doesn't have seven kids. Sometimes women would actually *like* it if their husbands obeyed them just like their kids did.

The relational harmony, seen in the unashamed nakedness seen in Genesis 2:25, is long gone at this point. But we have to understand that neither man nor women were cursed. If they were cursed, there would have been no coming back for them. No, the *ground* was cursed. Pain and complication were added *to the tasks* that God made them to accomplish. God didn't create work at the Fall, and He didn't lift His mandate to subdue and fill and rule the world.

God cursed *the ground* and introduced thorns into both Eve and Adam's work. Rather than working a blessed creation, after the Fall man had to toil over a cursed ground and he would have pain in his work all of his life. God's word of judgment against sin makes the work painful, the environment unwieldy, and relationships between men and women strained.

Because of sin, work will appear fruitless, it will appear futile, and it will take place in a fallen world. That's what I'm going to cover here. Work now appears fruitless, it appears futile, and it takes place in a fallen world. These are the thorns that I'm talking about, and that we struggle with every day of our lives.

The first two are connected: fruitfulness and futility. We'll consider them together.

Fruitfulness

Now, work is never actually fruitless, but the Fall broke us. We don't see it properly, and we are out of communion with God until God brings us back into the fold. Fruitfulness and futility are *perspective* issues. It's how we see things. They are not realities. They're something that combats our faith. These are thorns that attack the way we think about and the way we see our worlds. For so many of us, we are either opposed to work, or we make it an idol. I'm the one who's opposed to it. If I can get out of it, I will. All I've ever wanted was for someone to give me a severance package; to literally pay me to stop working. That's like a dream I have, but I don't think it's ever going to happen.

A lot of other people are workaholics. I am the way I am, I think, because my dad was a workaholic, so my rebellion drove me the other direction. But I think most of us fit into one of these two categories: either we want nothing to do with work, or we make an idol of work.

What do we mean when we say that work is fruitless? We mean that, in all of our work, we will be able to envision far more than we will accomplish— both because of a lack of ability, and because of resistance in the environment around us. The experience of work will include pain, conflict, envy, fatigue; and consequently, not all of our goals will be met. Your conflicts with others in the work environment will sap your confidence and undermine your productivity.

We daydream of what we would do if someone would just give us the opportunity. We aspire to greatness, to innovation, and to conquering the world. Right? We're Reconstructionists! We hear that word and we think, "Amen, brother, let's do this!" We all overestimate what we can do in the life that is given to us– or, we all underestimate what we can do. Either way, there is a fruitfulness problem that we have.

We envy other people's educations, their family connections, their stock options, their influence, their earning potential. We envy other people's fruitfulness and wonder where ours is. The funny thing is, the person that we generally envy is envying someone else. We look at how many kids someone else has and we wish we could have been more fruitful. Or we look at folks with fewer kids and think that somehow we could have been more fruitful without all the little resource suckers running around.

We struggle. We struggle with miscarriages and fertility issues. We get passed over for promotions. We don't get the job that we thought we were perfect for. We plan to bake and make a thousand things every day, and yet we never leave the laundry room or the schoolroom. My poor wife has plans like this– she would take over the world in a day, if somebody would just let her do it! But we've got these six kids and that tends to get in the way. I think all of you moms know exactly what I'm talking about!

We don't earn as much, we don't produce as much, we don't grow, our 401K doesn't grow, we aren't as spiritually mature as we hoped we would be, our friends and families aren't as spiritually mature as we thought... The lies mount, discouragement mounts, Satan twists us in knots with the staggering promises of God regarding fruitfulness, "Did God actually say?"

And where's the fruitfulness? He promises it in His word, and we want it *now*! Immediately! We want it fully and completely, without any trouble or labor!

The thorns and lies stab into our joy, drinking it up. The thorns and lies get tied around the axle of our minds, debilitating our momentum, progress, gratitude, and prayers. And because of God's intentions for our work– to contribute to the flourishing of the world– we have glimpses of what we can accomplish. But because of the Fall, our work is profoundly frustrating. It's never as fruitful as we want, and often it's even a complete failure.

This is why so many people inhabit the extremes of idealism or cynicism. Idealism says, "Through my work I'm going to change things, make a difference, accomplish something new, bring justice to the whole world." Cynicism says, "Nothing really changes. Don't get your hopes up. Do what it takes to make a living, but don't let yourself care too much. Get as much as you can while you can, and get out."

I work for the public sector in King County District Court, and I would say 100% of us are there just doing what we've gotta do until we can cash in that golden pension. I think this is why people get government jobs. I can testify to the truth of that.

We can be categorized as those who are overly enthusiastic about what we can accomplish if we work hard enough and are organized and dedicated enough (I won't make you raise your hands, but you know who you are.) Or, we fall into the other ditch of being so cynical that we hardly get out of bed in the morning– work is merely the path to retirement and true enjoyment. Fruitfulness doesn't matter, just get through.

For them, it's what Shakespeare said, "The world is but sound and fury, signifying nothing." Before I was a Christian that was a motto of mine. I had it put on a T-shirt: *"The world is but sound and fury, signifying nothing."*

Now, there are examples of the struggle with fruitfulness in the Bible. If we look there, we see Abraham, our great father. He was told that his seed would fill the earth like the stars of the heavens. In his lifetime, though, he had two marriages and the number of his children equalled the number of the constellation of Orion. And this is what we all deal with: we're promised the stars, but we can barely produce the constellation of Orion! And so we go back to Satan's temptation: Did God really say? Is God a liar? What is He doing? How is He doing it?

If we just look with our eyes and comprehend with our fallen minds, we will not get it. We will be frustrated, and we will see it as not just appearing to be fruitless, but we'll really think that and act accordingly.

Is the fulfillment of God's promise for Abraham's life methodical or incremental? Abraham has eight, Jacob has twelve, Joseph has two, and bada bing bada boom, you've got twenty-two by the end of Genesis. Twenty-two is a lot, right? It's more than Orion. It's not quite all the stars in the sky, but what you see in three generations is what you're getting here. The number of faithful who are waiting for the resurrection is a lot higher than it was when it was just Abraham. Eight to twelve to two, equaling twenty-two. We have bigger aspirations than that, don't we? But not God!

In the here and now, we struggle to see the bigger picture, to see beyond the horizon, to imagine what God might be accomplishing over time.

I have two friends I have known since I was 14. One is an extraordinarily successful doctor, the other is an extraordinarily successful Hollywood producer. They are wealthy, influential men, and they party a lot. These are friends I've had for a long time, and they are living life to the fullest, in their minds.

What I find fascinating is that when my wife and I go out to dinner with these two successful men– both unmarried in their 40s– I tend to envy them a little. I mean, here's all this money and power– and yet in an unguarded moment, I find out that *they* envy *me!* They are living Ecclesiastes! They see that it's coming to nothing! And here I am with a wife and six kids, building something for the future. The movies my friend makes? Nobody's going to remember them next year, let alone in 20 years, but by then I'll have grandkids.

That scenario for me is exactly how this works. Comparing ourselves to everyone else and the circumstance here and now totally gets us off the mark. It confuses us about the ultimate purposes of God. It's all a lie, and it's all the result of sin. It's just thorns gobbling us up, whipping us unexpectedly in the face.

Romans 8:20 says, "For the creation was subjected to futility…" Now the Oxford English Dictionary defines futility as "pointlessness or uselessness." When Adam sinned, the created world was also subjected to futility. Futility has more to do with what appears to be hopelessly impossible as our work seems ineffective in the larger world. One mom, one engineer, one preacher, one painter, one technician– what can they really accomplish in 80 years?

Alone, our work seems as pointless as charging into Hell with a squirt gun, like we're running into the flames, attempting to put them out with a little squirt gun. One thinks of more than just the thorns and thistles that are accompanying our work in Genesis 3:17-19, or the pain of childbirth. One thinks of the repeated refrain that "all is vanity" in Ecclesiastes.

Ecclesiastes, in the Septuagint– the Greek translation of the Old Testament– uses the same Greek word "futility" is the same Greek word Paul uses, which is why I believe he uses it. Creation was subjected to futility, the appearance of meaninglessness. Sin makes childbirth feel futile and instructing children seem futile.

How many of you have to tell your kid more than one time about everything? But what happens? We were wondering in the car on the way over here, "When did our kids stop doing that? That thing that was so annoying that other parents would tell us about, that their grandparents would tell us about? And when was the last time we even had to talk to them about it?" It felt like it was the only thing I had to talk to him about the first 11 years of his life!

At first it seems so futile. So pointless. My favorite story is about how I wanted to see how many times I washed this Pooh Bear cup my kids used. I stop counting at about 62 times. We literally washed Pooh Bear off of it. It's just a glass now. But in the moment, I was thinking, "I washed this cup this morning. I'm going to wash it later today. I'm washing it now. My whole life is washing this Pooh Bear cup."

If you're just living in this snapshot, go back to bed. What's the point? Nothing seems to last. Nothing seems permanent. Try weeding! The only permanent things seem to be change and decay. Work under the sun appears meaningless because it does not last. It takes away our hope in the future, alienates us from God and one another, and it takes away our joy in their presence. A little Pooh Bear cup takes away my joy in the living God!

We need some help here. This is the daily grind. This is the gospel. This is where we need help, because we are choking on our own sin, envy, and desire for what we could accomplish if God would just put us in the game. All of the thorns and thistles from outside are choking our work. This is the gospel. This is what we need help with.

Who is sufficient for these things? Who is going to free us from this body of death?

The two things I've covered so far are perspective issues: what is going on inside of us. If you leave the confines of your own heart and we go into the workplace, we find that it is just as fruitless and hostile and full of thorns as what is going on inside of us.

The Fallen Workplace

After the Fall, God said to the serpent, *"I will put enmity between you and the woman, between your offspring and her offspring. He shall bruise your head, and you shall bruise His heel."* (Genesis 3:15)

So there's a war. God put enmity between the children of Satan and the children of faith. We go into Genesis chapter 4 and we see this. In the first two boys born to Adam and Eve, you see the war He's talking about. There's the son of promise, and the son of cursing, and there's envy about the fruitfulness of their work. The son of cursing murders the son of promise. Welcome to the new garden.

When we consider the environment in which a Christian laborer works, it's more than the physical world that is

190

opposed to us. How many of you work in a strictly Christian company surrounded by Christians, nothing but a Christian worldview, nothing but Christian examples? Not many of us have that blessed reward. Not many of us toil somewhere where it's just Christian from top to bottom. Most of us go into a fallen world and work amongst the sons and daughters of Satan.

The Christian worker is constantly confronted by bad examples, within hearing of profanity and coarse joking and blasphemy. I can't even believe how much I hear blasphemy. I wonder, why would you bring Jesus into this conversation?

The Christian worker is subjected to gossip, slander, complaining, backbiting, malicious speech and lies. We're subjected to office smut which is always glamorized, marriage vows are broken and flirting is frivolous and wanton.

The Christian worker is subjected to immodest dress and seductive speech. He faces orders and expectations that require him to lie, to cheat, to steal, to deceive without information, and to present half truths as whole truths.

I work for a judge who has told me to lie on more than one occasion, and I've gone to my manager and said, "You'll have to get someone else to do this because I'm not going to do it." But it's a judge! If the judge is going to tell another person to lie, what kind of justice are they distributing? The court system doesn't need to be reformed, it needs to be reconstructed. We need to tear that thing down.

The Christian is surrounded by thorns at work because he does his work in the midst of Satan's traps and Satan's children. I worry very much about the men in my congregation. Some of them have to travel, some of them spend a lot of time in hotels alone, eating alone, driving alone, flying alone. Some people have to do that. That bothers me a lot about what might be going on there, because sin is everywhere. You go out into a world full of it.

The Christian worker must be mindful of the attacks of the enemy. Every situation has its own temptations and traps. Sitting down with your spouse and actually thinking about that, coming up with a list of things that you know are specific temptations and traps where you work is a very good idea.

But moms can hardly get time to get out of their housecoats, let alone to get out of the house, right? You know those days when you come home, husbands, and everyone is still in their pajamas? The kids always somehow think that's a triumph– and I just go over and hug my poor wife. Moms are surrounded by the needs of children, domestic maintenance, expectations that can drain all hope, self dignity, and joy.

Another thorn is that our motivations are also selfish. Ecclesiastes 4:4 says this: *Then I saw that all toil and all skill in work come from a man's envy of his neighbor.*

That's cynical, right there. All skill in work comes because one man is envious of another man? I believe it! But that's a sad state of affairs. So there's a constant tension at work. Do you feel that when you're at school, when you're at the park, the store, at work, when you're around unbelievers?

At my work, the gender benders, the misconceptions about justice, the average defendant easily inspires my compassion in Christian charity, actually. I feel a profound amount of compassion for the average defendant. I am tempted towards wrath and indignation towards my coworkers, however. I have discovered that I have no patience for impatient people, that I have no tolerance for intolerance. I look down on pride, and I curse foul language.

My real job must be logging, because I keep a ready supply of boards right here in my eyes. This is not something you were probably expecting me to say, but going into the workplace full of pagans shows that there are all kinds of thorns in our own hearts and minds. I have very little compassion for most of my coworkers because they are so self-righteous (I say self- righteously).

I could build a mansion in heaven for myself out of the logs jammed in my eye. Like the cedars of Lebanon are the sins jammed in my eyes.

So there's this tension all the time. I do have some Christian friends at work. We're a very tight knit group, and I praise God for that. We pray together, praise together, but given where I work, it's almost all women. The two Christians I work with are women. I'm very good friends with their husbands.

Now, the fear of man is so stark in some of your lives that you downplay your Christianity as much as you can. You probably have a list of curse words that you think are okay so you sound like anyone else.

The other ditch is the guy that is so joyless and mirthless, so self righteous and indignant about everything that nobody can stand him. But whatever the ditch is, the middle ground is courage. It's a war, and what warriors need is courage. C.S. Lewis said this about courage, though:

> "Courage is not simply one of the virtues, but the form of every virtue at the testing point, which means at the point of highest reality. "

Courage is the testing point of every other virtue. And that is what we all need, isn't it? To not be worried about the fear of man in one case is just saying what's true and standing up for what's right, but on the other hand, it's not fearing man and not being timid and holding back. It's a real struggle to be a good witness, to build relationships with people who are opposed to our God and all that He stands for.

Who can show us how to stand around the water cooler with the unbelieving coworker? Who has done this before? Who has shown compassion without compromise? The whole world was subjected to thorns, and waits for the revelation of the sons of God. We, too, wait for this revelation. How are we supposed to work in the midst of so many thorns?

In Genesis 3:15, God promised that a Son would come to deliver man from Satan, from sin, and from death, reversing the fall of man by restoring him, his relationships, and his work. Jesus is the greater Noah. This is what I'm going to explain here. We're going to look at Noah, and we're going to see how this promise starts in the early part of Genesis and is fulfilled in Jesus Christ.

Eve had this hope of a promised son right away when the first man was born to her, because the seed of the woman is supposed to be the deliverer. She said, "The Lord has given us a son."

But as we know, Cain was not by any stretch of the imagination the Redeemer that we were waiting for. And from that point on, all the sons of promise that were born, pointed to Christ. They served as types and shadows of the true Messiah. These Old Testament characters, the sons of promise, the prophecies about them, began to construct a theology of messiahship. They began to build the expectation of God's people.

The next major prophecy about the promised Redeemer came from Lamech, Noah's father. So you have Genesis 3:15, and it doesn't take very long before you start to see this messianic promise start to develop. I find this particular one is often overlooked, but it's so crucial to our everyday lives!

The term rendered "pain" in Genesis 3:16 and 3:17 occurs only three times in the Old Testament– only three times!– and is that pain that comes from our work. The other time, it's used is Genesis 5:29. All men and women experience this pain in their work, and at Noah's birth his father Lamech hoped that Noah will bring relief from this painful toil.

> Genesis 5:28-29 says: *And Lamech lived a hundred eighty and two years, and begat a son: And he called his name Noah, saying, This same shall comfort us concerning our work and toil of our hands, because of the ground which the Lord hath cursed.*

A man would come from the dirt. The word "adam" means dirt. A man would come from the dirt— true humanity– who would deliver mankind from the curse of the thorns and its pain, restoring fruitfulness, and freeing us to fulfill the cultural mandate to subdue, rule, and fill the earth of God with our restored work.

Now, Noah is a type of Jesus in that he carried a new humanity safely through the waters of cleansing to new life. Peter used that example: Jesus is like Noah because he carries the faithful through the waters of promise into righteousness.

It is fascinating to me that the first promises of the Messiah that come after the first generation of humans are promises about deliverance from the thorns that make our work so painful. Think about that! The thing that Lamech wanted deliverance from was the thorns, because in his mind the thorns represent the fallen state of man. Calvin explained the connection in his commentary wonderfully:

The Jews do not judge erroneously in declaring Lamech's expression to be a prophecy; but they are too gross in restricting to agriculture what is applicable to all those miseries of human life which proceed from the curse of God, and are the fruits of sin. I come, indeed, to this conclusion: that the holy fathers anxiously sighed, when, being surrounded with so many evils they were continually reminded of the first origin of all evils, and regarded themselves as under the displeasure of God.

Therefore in the expression, the toil of our hands, there is the figure synecdoche; because under one kind of toil he comprises the whole miserable state into which mankind had fallen. For they undoubtedly remembered what Moses has related above, concerning the laborious, sad, and anxious life to which Adam had been doomed: and since the wickedness of man was daily increasing, no mitigation of the penalty could be hoped for, unless the Lord should bring unexpected succor. It is probable that they were very earnestly looking for the mercy of God; for their faith was strong, and necessity urged them ardently to desire help.

It was their toil, it was their work! They would go in and thorns would come at them from every angle! It reminds them every single day that the curse is not the work itself, but the *difficulty* of it. The pain. The thorns. We are people laboring under a curse.

Lamech's comment on the name 'Noah,' which, strictly speaking, means 'rest', also introduces the related concept of comfort. Lamech expected that Noah would bring both rest and comfort from the painful toil of work that daily reminds us of the curse, the Fall, and the state of rebellion and judgment under which man has fallen.

But this is all ultimately fulfilled in Christ. Noah is a long way from the true Messiah, but think about how Paul describes Jesus in 2 Corinthians 1:3-5:

> *Praise be to the God and Father of our Lord Jesus Christ, the Father of compassion and the God of all comfort, who comforts us in all our troubles, so that we can comfort those in any trouble with the comfort we ourselves receive from God. For just as we share abundantly in the sufferings of Christ, so also our comfort abounds through Christ.*

It wasn't *Noah* that Lamech really wanted to come. It was *Christ* that he was waiting for! Ultimately, Lamech was prophesying about the coming of Jesus Christ. As we share in Christ's sufferings, as we exchange our iniquity for His righteousness, as we take up our cross, enduring the enmity of Satan and Satan's children, as we clothe ourselves in Christ, sharing in His death and resurrection, Jesus comforts us.

Receiving comfort does not mean that we find ourselves without troubled circumstances, but in the midst of our troubled circumstances, we find the profound wellbeing that comes from resting in God's sovereignty and mercy. A concept first expressed by the Hebrew word "shalom" is translated as "peace" in John 14:27:

> *Peace I leave with you; my peace I give you. I do not give to you as the world gives. Do not let your hearts be troubled and do not be afraid.*

Why, because now the thorns are magically gone? No, because He has overcome the world! If we take up our cross and follow Him, in Him we overcome the world. In Him, the thorns have no power over us.

Noah was a lesser Jesus, Jesus is a greater Noah. Jesus enters our work and comforts us, gives us peace and courage in the midst of it, cutting back the thorns that frustrate our labor. Reading the Bible, praying, going to church, enjoying fellowship– these are the means with which God gives us comfort in the midst of our circumstances. Psalm 23:5 says, "He sets a table in the midst of our enemies." What is a table? A table is a place of comfort, a place of resting, a place of communion, a place where you feast, a place where you gather strength. And He's taken that table of victory and placed it right smack in the middle of our enemies!

Jesus, the God-man, came to the earth born of Mary. He is the Lord of the Sabbath, the Lord of rest. He took upon His head the crown of thorns because He took the result of the curse upon Himself. The symbol is not just a symbol. It's not an accident that they put thorns on His head, because He takes the fruit of the curse, the thorns that frustrate us every single day, and put it on His forehead. "I will take this curse upon Me." That is what the Gospel is!

Jesus doesn't free us from work, he frees us to work as we were made to work. He restores work to its proper end, because He's taking care of the thorns. Work isn't our punishment. Working under the curse of futility and frustrated faithfulness is our punishment. Estrangement from our co-laborers, our fellow man, our spouse, the very ground– this estrangement is reversed by Jesus because He deals with the sin.

Most Christians operate under the belief that the good life, the Christian life is one freed from the curse of work, freed from burden, from difficulty, from strenuous labor. But the curse is the fruit of sin, estrangement from our mission of fruitfulness. Both subduing and filling require work– even strenuous work. Think about it. Before the Fall, God said,

"Go and subdue it. Go guard and keep the garden." Does that sound easy?

Freedom from the curse isn't getting to a place where nothing is difficult to do. Work is difficult enough without the thorns! He says, "Hey! My yolk is light," you know why? Because it doesn't have thorns. He just has the work. Have you ever wondered why He said that? Because there's no curse! He labors without it! And in Him, you, too, labor without it.

The point is not that when the seed of the woman triumphs over the serpent, man will be relieved from work altogether; but rather, that God's judgment on man's work will be removed! God spoke judgment over man's work in response to man's sin. If the sin is removed, so, too, are the effects of the judgment. Work for us is liberated.

The King who wore the crown of thorns is the King who liberates us from the curse of thorns. He worked diligently and cheerfully. He was compassionate, and giving, and merciful. His will was the Father's will. The Father's will was his food. Jesus is the example of the Christian worker: a selfless servant who did all things well. He didn't envy anyone. He didn't think equality with God was something to be grasped and taken and stolen and roughed out of His Father's hands. He had compassion. He had joy. His labor, his yoke, was light, because all it was, was work itself. If we look to work as a means to fill the deep hole in our hearts, the longing for material security, for purpose, for worth, and for respect, work will never fill us up. It will be a selfish idol. Blaise Pascal, in his work Pensées, says this:

> What else does this craving, and this helplessness, proclaim but that there was once in man a true happiness, of which all that now remains is the empty print and trace? This he tries in vain to fill with everything around him, seeking in things that are not

there the help he cannot find in those that are, though none can help, since this infinite abyss can be filled only with an infinite and immutable object; in other words by God himself.

Your work cannot satisfy you in itself. Your work cannot fill you. Your work cannot give you purpose or meaning. *He* does. He fills you. He gives you purpose. He gives you a reason to go and do work. The most successful people I know are people who take or leave the work. Give them Christ! And with Christ they labor under His rule and reign and in His comfort, and they succeed far more than people without it. When I say "successful people" I'm not talking about rich people. I'm talking about well rounded, God-fearing, happy families. People who have it all together are people who are laboring not under the curse, but under Christ.

Jesus liberates us from the curse of thorns so that we can imitate the Creator from Genesis 1, in whose image we were created. Right? It says we were created in His image, and if you go back and look, it never describes what His image is. It just says from start to finish, in Genesis 1 and 2, that he worked. That's the image we're given, a worker. God worked and then rested from His work. And we are made in that image, and that's what we're restored to.

Matthew 11:25-30: *At that time Jesus answered and said, I thank thee, O Father, Lord of heaven and earth, because thou hast hid these things from the wise and prudent, and hast revealed them unto babes. Even so, Father: for so it seemed good in thy sight. All things are delivered unto me of my Father: and no man knoweth the Son, but the Father; neither knoweth any man the Father, save the Son, and he to whomsoever the Son will reveal him. Come unto me, all ye that labour and are heavy laden, and I will give you rest. Take my yoke upon you, and learn of me; for*

I am meek and lowly in heart: and ye shall find rest unto your souls. For my yoke is easy, and my burden is light.

God has revealed Himself to little children– His little children, the sons and daughters of God– that earth, suffering under the curse, is longing to be revealed. Jesus comes and makes us children of God. He frees us from our thorns by wearing them. He gives us the rest that our souls long for, not from work, but from the curse. He gives us peace and courage, and as we are revealed as the sons of God, we fight back against the thorns of the curse in every vocation that we are called into. We forgive sins and we seek forgiveness, and we see that that particular electric hedge trimmer is powerful enough to get through the vine. Right? When you forgive other people's sins and you seek forgiveness, what happens is that the curse begins to diminish all around you.

Come to the Father through Jesus, come to the humble and gentle King, in whose hand everything rests. Bring your labors, every hour of every day, and there lay them, and find the rest that you seek– not from *work*, but from the *curse*. Rest in Him and your yoke will become light, for He will carry it as He carries you.

Let's pray:

Father God, I pray that everyone here would go forth, believing and trusting in You; knowing that You are the Lord and the sovereign of this world and of the entire cosmos.

I pray for everyone here, Father. You know that we are sinners, you know that we suffer. You know the thorns that choke our work and our hope, faith, and joy. I pray, Father God, that in Christ You would continue to work through us, to strengthen us in our faith and our understanding of Your word; that we would obey because we love you. That we would go forth and cut back the thorns that choke our work.

In Christ we are victorious, and I pray that everyone here would rest in Jesus Christ as they go to work tomorrow morning, and that they would see the thorns being pushed back by our Lord and our Savior, in whose name we pray.

Amen.

Part III

Woman of Virtue

Loving Your Husband as He Fulfills His Calling

By Susan Eby

The hauntingly beautiful bagpipe music of the song "Highland Cathedral" filled the spring air as I gazed through the trees that lined the vineyard on that gorgeous May afternoon, eager to capture my first glimpse of the bride– my daughter. And suddenly, there she was– beautiful and graceful on the arm of my husband Dan, who struggled visibly to keep tears from surfacing. Clearly, he sensed at that moment– like I did– that something hugely significant was happening in our lives.

They turned a corner, and with the crescendo of the music, regally made their way up the outdoor aisle to the rustic, floral-covered arch ahead of us where her bridegroom waited for her.

Then this was the part where the pastor was supposed to say, "Who gives this woman to this man?" and Dan would undoubtedly have replied, "Her mother and I do," before he stepped back, probably kissed her, and took his seat beside me.

But that's not what happened.

No one was more surprised than I was when the pastor handed his microphone to Dan, and Dan proceeded to address the groom:

"Jason Bradford Rose, this is the day that you have been waiting for. But in fact, it's the day that Susan and I have been preparing for, for many years. Sons leave home, but daughters are given.

A son leaves his father and mother in order to take a wife and establish a new home. A daughter is given to a young man who is ready to establish a home. The purpose of the Lord is for godly families to be established on the earth. We see that in Genesis 18, where Abram was to command his children in the way of the Lord. It is for this purpose that your parents, Jim and Barbara, prepared you, their son.

The book of Malachi communicates the purpose of a godly home in which two become one– to raise godly seed. God is seeking families to be established on the earth who will raise godly children. This is the burden that we, Sarah's parents, carried: to prepare a daughter fit for the man who has responded to this high calling.

I stand here today at the threshold of this new covenant of marriage that is about to be established. I am ready to relinquish my duties as Sarah's father, as her protector and covering, and give her hand to you in marriage, so that in agreeing to this covenant, you become her protector, her covering, her husband. While it has been my duty to care for, nourish and protect Sarah as her father, you now take on these duties as her husband. I conclude my responsibility with a charge and a blessing:

To you, Jason– take up with joy this high calling of a husband. Rejoice in the wife of your youth. Protect her, provide for her, lead her, and love her in all godliness.

To you, Sarah– gladly follow Jason as your husband, submitting to his leading. Pray for him, encourage him, assist him in embracing the vocations to which God calls him.

To both of you– establish a godly home. Embrace the privilege of having children, and joyfully take on the burden of raising godly children, as this is the purpose of two becoming one– the ultimate purpose being to glorify God.

I bless you!"

Then he kissed Sarah, hugged Jason, and sat down beside me. And at that moment, what had just happened in our lives became very, very clear.

Truthfully, for a long time, I had struggled over the traditional *"...her mother and I..."* part of the ceremony. I didn't want Dan to include it in Sarah's wedding ceremony– certainly not because I felt any less involved than Dan was in bringing Sarah to this turning point in her life! Without a doubt, as a mother I had been completely in the saddle with my husband in our child-rearing. Both of us had taught and trained our children. Both had taken turns sitting up at night with croupy kids. Both of us had participated in the ups and downs of raising them. Both of us had rushed to the ER in grief when we found out she had been seriously injured in a horrific car accident. Both of us had shared responsibilities in educating the kids. Both of us had cared for and encouraged and nourished and disciplined. And both of us had blessed this new marriage.

But my hesitation was because I knew that my role and Dan's had distinct differences that each of us would ultimately be accountable to God for. His, not mine, was the burden and the role of protector, provider, and spiritual covering. Except in the case of my husband's death or abandonment, as a woman I should not have to carry such a heavy load.

My role was to bear, train, teach, nurture my young, and assist my husband in every way as we brought our family purpose to completion. It was my husband's name that our daughter carried, typifying his protection and covering over her, until the moment of this covenant transfer where she took on her husband's name in acknowledgment of his role as her new protector, provider, leader.

Unity of the Husband and Wife

Genesis recounts the story of God creating man. As the story unfolds, man was given a distinct responsibility. More than merely exercising stewardship over God's creation, he was given the task of governing it:

"Be fruitful and multiply, and fill the earth and subdue it, and have dominion over the fish of the sea and over the birds of the heavens and over every living thing that moves on the earth" (Genesis 1:28.) This command was repeated to Noah after the flood, and again to the exiles of Israel when they were in Babylon.

Man was commanded by God to subdue *[that is, "to tame; to conquer"]* and to have dominion over *[that is, to "govern"]* God's creation as representatives of the Creator, and to dress and keep the garden in which he was created. In order that he might accomplish this role, God made woman to be his help. After saying so many times, "God saw that it was good," suddenly in Genesis 2:18 God said that it was *not* good that man should be alone. *"I will make him a help suitable for him."*

Adam was alone, but he was not lonely. How could he possibly have felt lonely when God himself communed with him every day? But Adam had a huge task given to him, and in order to fully accomplish it, he needed someone to help him in a suitable, qualified way. Together, they shared common goals. Together, they moved ahead to accomplish the work that they were given to do.

So it is in a godly marriage relationship, that the husband and wife together form a unit whereby their combined efforts propel the relationship forward into what they are called by God to accomplish.

The Bible points us to pictures in life that help to illuminate Christ, and give greater understanding of Who He is– and marriage is one of the pictures the Bible speaks of.

> *"The husband is the head of the wife even as Christ is the head of the church, his body... Now as the church submits to Christ, so also wives should submit in everything to their husbands. Husbands, love your wives as Christ loved the church and gave himself up for her... Therefore, a man shall leave his father and mother and hold fast to his wife, and the two shall become one flesh. This mystery is profound, and I am saying that it refers to Christ and the church"* *(Ephesians 5:22 forward.)*

Somehow in our current culture, too often Christians have been swept right along with non-Christians into distorting the picture of Christ's protection and provision over His Bride the Church, as women have sought to compete, to prove that they are equal – or better yet, superior– to men in intelligence, strength, and ability. Consequently, women are independently entering arenas, even in the church, where they are being required to take on great burdens that they were never intended to carry, of protecting, providing, and defending.

Yet to blur these lines of distinction between a man and a woman is to resist the very creative order that God ordained in order to represent the distinction of Christ (the husband) and the Church (the wife.) In a truly amazing testimony of God's wisdom, these roles are built right into our DNA, creating perfect harmony when the man and the woman fulfill their God-ordained distinctions. You've seen His creative order reflected in your young children.

It fascinates me to see it so evident! Several years ago, I spontaneously took a grandson with me to do some errands, and he didn't have time to change his dress-up clothes. At three, Ethan was small for his age anyway, and it just hadn't occurred to me how funny such a tiny person looked with a police hat that was too big and a dress-up uniform that said POLICE across his back. Immediately, it drew the attention of dozens of shoppers, starting with the staff attendant at the front door at Costco. "Are *you* a policeman?" he asked. Right away, Ethan responded to the attention authoritatively and said so seriously, "I'm the sheriff! I'm looking for the bad guys!"

How is it that my grandsons would instinctively thrive in filling roles of "protector/provider," pretending to be hunters, police officers, intergalactic warriors…while my granddaughters instinctively love frilly dresses and want to be mothers or princesses? Years ago, I caught my own young sons using one of my daughter's dolls as a football, and yet I found her snuggling their stiff "C3PO" (Star Wars robot) action figure, all wrapped up in a blanket.

God's Law is written on our hearts, and His Law has a far higher and more perfect purpose than man can ever conceive of. Just as His Law promises blessings for obedience and curses for disobedience, we are currently witnessing the complete chaos and restlessness– the "curse"– of disobedience to His Law in our culture today.

Ironically, a woman's worth and value are never diminished in the least if she cannot or does not fulfill the same role that her husband has been given to do. On the contrary! A complete whole is created when the husband and wife respect and fulfill their individual God-ordained roles. Together, they form a strong unity. Proverbs 31 says,

*"Her husband trusts in her, and he will have no lack of gain. She does him good, and not harm all the days of her life...**Strength and dignity** are her clothing..."*

Does that sound like a woman who's suppressed?

No, I didn't think so either.

The Foundation: "What do you believe?"

As you know, marriage these days is under horrific attack, and you're undoubtedly assuming that when someone's been married for as long as I have, there *must* be helpful little nuggets of wisdom, or maybe "Ten Steps to Loving Your Husband as He Fulfills His Calling" that I could share with you, right? There *are* good ideas out there, to be sure! But the truth is, there's something else that's far more fundamental– and necessary– for us to consider when we're looking at how to become the God pleasing wife who will be a strength, support, and suitable help to her husband in his calling. Let me give you an example of what I mean:

When Dan and I began to educate our children, the first thing we automatically started to look for was a good, solid curriculum. The first thing we wanted to know was, *"What do we **do**?"* But thankfully, very early on a friend challenged us to consider that what was far more important for us to determine before anything else at all– including the curriculum– was, *"What do we **believe**?"*

What were the fundamental, non-negotiable things that we believe, by which all facts are to be comprehended? What was "the plumb line" by which we would measure everything we learned and taught? That is, what was our ***worldview***- that lens of faith through which we viewed all of life? *That's* the foundation that education is build upon, and *everything else* – including curriculum–would spring from that one thing.

In just the same way, God-pleasing marriages don't come from simply following patterns, steps, or other women's experiences or advice, as good as they may be, but from **what you believe** –from your **worldview.** Patterns and ideas –the "curriculum," if you will– always follow worldview. Always. Worldview shapes the structure.

Right now, far too many distorted ideas about marriage are pushing hard against biblical belief constantly. For good or for bad, every marriage is solely the result of what the individual believes about these three things, which form the basis of *every* worldview:

1. Who is God?

2. Who is man?

3. Which of them has the ultimate authority– the final word– on anything?

For instance, can a woman really end the life of the baby in her womb because it's *her* body? Can she rightfully choose to be euthanized because it's *her* own life she's ending? Is it okay if she leaves her marriage when it isn't making *her* happy anymore? Can she change the order and structure of her marriage because *she's* just as intelligent and gifted as her husband is? In fact, can she self-identify as a man because *she* feels more comfortable that way? Should we even care, or should we assume that since it's her life, she can do with it as she wants to?

Worldview directs every one of these situations, and multitudes more. And every worldview is powered by the individual's faith. Have you noticed that in trying to bring order out of the present chaos of our culture, conservative politicians often urge Americans to become "people of faith"– then quickly add, "whatever your faith might be." But the fact is, we already *are* a people of faith. Everybody has "faith," just as everybody has a worldview. The big question is, faith in *whom*?

R.J. Rushdoony once wrote:

> *"Ours is a great age of faith, but not in Christ... Our problem is not a lack of faith, but too much false faith. True faith is to believe in Jesus Christ; it is to believe that God is, and that He is a rewarder of them that diligently seek him... If our faith rests on any other foundation than the triune God and His redeeming power through Christ, it is false."*

A friend of mine was battling Stage 4 cancer and eternity seemed imminent for her. Though she'd grown up in a Christian home, there didn't seem to be any evidence of Christian faith in her life, so in conversation I was very, very relieved to hear her say emphatically, "We just have to have *faith...!"*

That wasn't a phrase she typically used, so to hear her say it definitely caught my attention! *"Yes!"* I thought, as in my mind I fist-pumped both my arms, *"This is awesome!"* But just as quickly, my heart took a dive as she continued in the same breath, "...we just have to *believe in ourselves!"*

And, alas, there was the rub. Her faith in man– not in God– was forming a humanist worldview, where man was at the center. "Man" was her god, and held the final authority–had the last word– on everything. And that's exactly how she was living her life. The trouble is, trusting in man is worshipping the creature instead of the Creator that Romans 1:25 warns us about, and yet this is the very idea that forms the humanist faith that dominates our culture right now– both in and out of church.

Can you grasp the reality of this foolishness? Trusting the creature instead of the Creator is like the half-inch-long fetus in utero– still in the process of being shaped and formed, and still so far from what it will be– challenging the ideas of his mother against his own, disqualifying her because she isn't the same size and shape as he currently is.

Whether man likes it or not, there is a higher authority– a creative order– that man must submit to, in order to dispel chaos. All things were created by Him and for Him, and in Him all things hold together (Col.1:16-17)– whether we choose to acknowledge it or not.

In our current culture, the greatest conflict we're facing in marriages today is this clash of opposing world views. False faith that manifests itself in an "anthropocentric" *(i.e. man-centered)* worldview– humanism– erroneously believes that man holds ultimate authority, and it has foolishly declared all out war against a firm "Theocentric" *(i.e. God-centered)* worldview that affirms the truth that God holds ultimate authority. It's a declaration of warfare against God Himself.

It's the battle over the very definition and purpose of marriage as God defined it for His own purpose and glory, over the roles of men and women within marriage, and over who has the final word on *any*thing. It's not new, of course.

R.C. Sproul once said that:

> *"Humanism was not invented by man, but by a snake who suggested that the quest for autonomy might be a good idea."*

Let's address, for a minute, the primary excuse for any perversion in any relationship. I can pretty much guarantee that you've heard someone use the argument, "I can't help *[name the perversion]*. I was born this way!" For instance, "I'm lesbian, I was born this way." " I can't help being bossy, I was born this way." "I can't help gossiping, I was born this way…" There is no point trying to argue that a lesbian *wasn't* born that way, because truthfully, she believes she has been. The only truth that matters is that the biblical reality of "who man is" reinforces to us that we are, indeed, born in sin. Every one of us. But that doesn't *excuse* sin.

Because an individual may have particular tendencies toward sin– whether lesbian leanings, or disrespect toward one's husband, or the urge to usurp his authority– we cannot condone the sin or justify it or accept it as valid just because we believe we were born that way. Sin is sin even if it was evidenced from birth, and must be repented of, and turned away from by the grace and help of Almighty God.

In Christian circles, sin can be so attractively dressed up in such a way that it actually appears beautiful. Christian women often take on the roles that God has assigned– for good reason– to men even within the church, because they believe they are just as intelligent, gifted, and able to hear from God as men are. They were *born* that way. And yet this not only defies the picture of Christ and the Church that is supposed to be a perpetual testimony to the world through the witness of male/female role distinctions, but it also contributes, inadvertently, to the growing divide–the intense competition– between men and women in our current culture.

Okay, I know what you're thinking. You're thinking, like I am, that obviously *your* worldview *is* God-centered. Seriously, it's hard for me to imagine that I would so easily surrender to ideas that are wrong, given the right circumstances. We assume we'd stand strong against what offends God, measured by the standard of what His Word says. But too often, Christians 'think' we believe in a God-centered worldview and yet we find ourselves sometimes sliding into a dichotomy, where our faith applies to only *some* areas, but not others.

We see the importance of God-centered faith, of course– but in reality, many times we're not really paying attention to it and consequently we slide into "man-centered" thinking or action. We know what God-centered faith is, but unless we embrace the reality that true faith applies to *every* area of life with no exceptions, humbly dependent on the Holy Spirit to enlighten us, and are steeped in His fixed, unchanging Law– the Bible– we will miss it over and over, sliding into man-centered thinking again.

Here's a sobering example: Del Tackett *(of "The Truth Project")* once related the story of a Christian man who came to him for help in overcoming his addiction to pornography. After hearing him out for awhile, Mr. Tackett said, "Okay, I see the problem: I see that you don't really believe in an ever-present God."

The man strongly disagreed. "Oh no! That's not my problem at all!" he insisted. "My problem isn't with my *faith*. My problem is *pornography*! I *do* believe in an ever-present God!"

"Well… no, you don't," Mr. Tackett continued. "You just told me that the most difficult time for you to resist your urge to watch pornography is when your wife leaves the house and you are 'alone.'"

The man, though a Christian, was wife-conscious, but not God-conscious. Not really. In his thinking, his *faith* was separate from his *problem*. He did not, in fact, have a comprehensive Biblical worldview, a God-focused lens of true faith which has something to say about every aspect of his life, with no exceptions. His life was divided into compartments whereby his faith only applied to some areas, but not others.

Our own weaknesses and sins may not be the same as this man's, but we have to admit that there are areas of our lives in which we too, just like this Christian man, too easily slide away from being "God-focused," right into being man-focused.

And lest we think we can't be deceived, consider the disciples– those men who were physically with Jesus 24/7. After so much time together, at one point He asked them (in Mark 8:27-29), "Who do you say that I am?" Simple question, right? But… they didn't really know.

Most of them were focused on great men of the past, because "man" was their only point of reference, the only way they could measure anything. They wondered if maybe he was John the Baptist, or Elijah, or Jeremiah, or one of the prophets. But only Simon Peter answered correctly, "You are the Christ, the Son of the Living God!" At that moment, Peter "saw" who Jesus really was.

Yet only a few verses later, when Jesus began telling His disciples that He must go to Jerusalem and suffer many things from the elders and chief priests, be killed, and rise on the third day, Peter, emotionally distraught over what he was hearing, took Jesus aside to rebuke him, basically saying, "No way! There's no way *we're* going to let that happen to *you!*"

Jesus had just said that Peter's name was like "The Rock" upon which He would build His church– and yet now, merely minutes later, he said to him, "Get behind me, Satan! You are a hindrance to me. For you are not setting your mind on the things **of God**, but on the things **of man**!"

Just like Peter, we too will sometimes fail– but we know what our goal is and our desire is to pursue it. God has called us into a comprehensive *Theo*centric faith, into a Kingdom that far, far surpasses that of man! The Kingdom of God is so much greater than this world– and yet it touches every part of it.

Serving Our Husbands, Our Families, the Household of God

And ironically, as women, we are called by God to actively live out this great faith primarily through serving those who are right here, right in front of our faces– our husbands, our families, those in the household of faith.

Psalm 101:2 says, *"I will walk with integrity **within my house**."* These are some of the most convicting words I know of! It's in our homes and with our families that the genuineness of true faith is tested, refined, and purified. As wives, our deepest desire is to glorify God as we live out our faith by loving our husbands, assisting them in their vocations as we bring our family purpose to fulfillment.

We must also remember– and constantly encourage each other to remember– that this Kingdom which we are part of is so much more than us and our own marriage. This seems so obvious, and yet it's one of the primary weaknesses that Christians wives fall into! Let me explain it like this:

My husband Dan plays the bass guitar, and some time ago, he was asked to participate in a beautiful, full orchestral arrangement of Easter music. During the performance, I sat in the audience mesmerized by the beauty of... *the bass guitar!* Foolishly, because of my love for Dan, all I could hear was the bass guitar, and myopic, I fell into believing it was the most amazing part of the performance.

218

It seemed to me as though the bass was the "star of the show," until in one single moment, the breathtaking fullness of the whole performance swept over me with such force that I was stunned with the obvious revelation that Dan's bass guitar was, in fact, only one of many, *many* beautiful instruments privileged to share together in such a majestic creation of music bringing glory to God!

God's Story was being exalted through the many musicians, each doing his/her part, working together, and culminating in a complete whole that was so beautiful as it pointed to Jesus Christ! All the parts were necessary; all the parts shared in the joy of glorifying God.

In exactly the same way, our individual marriage is not the star of the show. God is. Just like every participant in this orchestra who was fulfilled in doing his part, somehow God has chosen us along with many others to participate together with Him in creating a beautiful masterpiece of music, like supporting actors who all do their part and share together in weaving a story He is writing that illuminates the true Star. Through flawed and imperfect people, His Story, His Song, brings glory to Him.

Like I was at the performance, too often we tend to become myopic in our own marriages, as though it was all about us. When we inadvertently find ourselves sliding into the man-centered worldview, we find ourselves either jealously coveting the seeming success of other marriages, or criticizing them. We feel the pride of success if our marriage seems good, and feel deep failure if it doesn't. We complain if our expectations aren't met, or our ideals aren't accomplished, or our needs aren't gratified. We compete, we compare ourselves with others, we judge others self-righteously. We tear down– or we worship and idolize. Do we measure ourselves against *other marriages*, instead of against Scripture?

God-centered women understand that, along with all the other Godly marriages that surround us, together we are all on the same team, participants in the same orchestra, each couple playing their role as part of the whole to the glory of God. God's glory is our passionate desire, our goal, our hope, our driving motivation. Our great desire must be for the success of *all* the Godly marriages around us. What a blessing to be counted among such a group, to be part of this "orchestra!"

Just imagine a musician beside you struggling with the music in the orchestra. For the success of the performance, you would seek to help and correct the struggling musician to fine- tune his music. If one instrument is out of tune, it will affect the whole symphony! This is not a time for the other musicians to gloat over how well they themselves are doing their own part, pleased that they aren't out of tune like that other instrument is. Discord in the music immediately takes the attention away from the whole performance, and the listeners are left focusing on the what went wrong. Instead, those observing from the outside ought to be swept up in the beauty of the overall masterpiece that points to the true star of the performance, the breathtaking music created by everyone beautifully performing their individual roles.

If Christians marriages fail, it's the name of Christ that suffers. If Christian marriages succeed, it's the name of Christ that's glorified. And that ought to be music to our ears!

Wives, you are here today– both individually and collectively– in order to be encouraged and strengthened for the task. The call of God on your life as a wife is to love your husband in the call of God on *his* life.

There's a wonderful charge given to husbands and wives in Ephesians 5, when the chapter ends with this amazing command:

"Let each one of you [husbands] love his wife as himself, and let the wife see that she respects her husband."

Wives, do you truly understand the powerful impact of a wife's respect toward your husband? This powerful combination of love and respect toward each other is something the world cannot understand. It's peace in the midst of chaos. It's order in the midst of disorder. It's purpose in the midst of restlessness. It's a high calling in the midst of cultural emptiness.

My responsibility as an older woman is to encourage you, as Titus 2 says, to "love your husband" in his calling and vocation. The word "love" is one that we wives are obliged to often consider, *especially* in this current culture where it's likely the most misused and misrepresented word in our vocabulary! Romans 12: 9 urges us to make sure that love is genuine, without hypocrisy. That is, to "abhor what is evil; cleave to what is good."

C.S. Lewis once wrote that, *"Being in love is not merely a feeling..."* Okay, we all know that by now. We know that "romance" is only the gift wrap– it's attractive, enticing, and it's what God has designed to draw us into the relationship– but it's not the treasure, which is far deeper, far more satisfying, and infinitely more valuable.

My granddaughter Sadie was not quite two when her Uncle Justin was married. After Justin and Anne returned from their honeymoon, our family met together at our house to watch them open their wedding gifts, but as we all went into the family room, we were shocked to see that little Sadie had already started tearing into the gifts! Fascinated by the wrapping, she was going from one to the next, totally drawn to the beautifully decorated boxes. But once each gift was open, she had no interest in the actual gift, and went on to the next pretty package.

Sadie was acting like a toddler. Unfortunately, there are far too many grown women who regard marriage the same way. And yet we know that we cannot depend on feelings– the external romance– to sustain us because they're too unpredictable and unstable.

But Lewis continued:

> *"...[love] is a deep unity, maintained by the will, and deliberately strengthened by habit, reinforced by the grace which both partners ask, and receive, from God."*

The most powerful way in which we, as wives, can stand firm against the enemies of God in this current cultural warfare that is seeking to destroy marriage as God defined it, to scoff at your role as a Godly wife assisting and helping your husband in his calling, is to maintain the strong unity of the husband and wife as God commanded in His creative order. Stand firm.

R. J. Rushdoony wrote:

> *"The Scripture gives no ground whatsoever to the idea that a marriage can be terminated when love ends. While love is important to a marriage, it cannot replace God's law as the essential bond of marriage."*

It's this unity, maintained by the will, reinforced by God's grace, that will equip you to assist your husband as he pursues his God-given vocation.

In his book, "Visions of Vocation," Steve Garber noted that the word 'vocation' is a rich one. He defined the word beautifully right at the beginning as *"... the wholeness of life, the range of relationships and responsibilities. Work, yes, but also families, and neighbors, and citizenship...**that to which***

I am called as a human being living my life before the face of God."

Understanding that, consider what R.J. Rushdoony wrote,

> *"...While marriage is the ordained sexual relationship between man and woman, it cannot be understood simply in terms of sex. When marriage is reduced to sex, then marriage disintegrates as an institution and amoral sex replaces it. Marriage has reference first of all to God's ordination and then to man and to woman in their respective callings. Because man is to be understood in terms of his calling under God, all of man's life is to be interpreted in terms of this calling too. Dislocation in a man's calling is a dislocation in his total life...*

> *"...Whether retired or actively working, a man's thinking is still in terms of the world of work, and he continues to assess reality in the same terms. Man, having been called to exercise dominion through work, is tied to work in thought and action alike. But there is no true dominion for man in and through work apart from God and His law-order."*

So in understanding this, wives, how is it that we can love our husbands in that to which they are called, living their lives before the face of God? What *is* the "curriculum" that follows belief? When Dan and I were married back in the '70s, we chose Colossians 3 for the foundation of the pastor's message that has sustained us through many years, and I was incredibly blessed when one of our sons and daughters-in-law chose the same scripture at their wedding. Consider this as it applies to your calling as a wife toward your husband:

"If then you have been raised with Christ, seek the things that are above, where Christ is, seated at the right hand of God. Set your minds on things that are above, not on things that are on earth. For you have died, and your life is hidden with Christ in God. When Christ who is your life appears, then you also will appear with him in glory.

Put to death therefore what is earthly in you: sexual immorality, impurity, passion, evil desire, and covetousness which is idolatry... But now you must put them all away: anger, wrath, malice, slander, and obscene talk from your mouth. Do not lie to one another, seeing that you have put off the old self with its practices and have put on the new self, which is renewed in knowledge after the image of its creator...

Put on then, as God's chosen ones, holy and beloved, compassionate hearts, kindness, humility, meekness, and patience, bearing with one another and if one has a complaint against another, forgiving each other as the Lord has forgiven you... Let the peace of Christ rule in your hearts...Let the word of Christ dwell in you richly, teaching and admonishing one another in all wisdom, singing psalms and hymns and spiritual songs with thankfulness in your hearts to God. And whatever you do, in word or deed, do everything in the name of the Lord Jesus, giving thanks to God the Father through him. Wives, submit to your husbands as is fitting in the Lord. Husbands, love your wives..."

And now let's go back to that beautiful spring day in the orchard so long ago. As my husband had urged our daughter Sarah on her wedding day so long ago, this is exactly the same charge for you as you leave here. Ladies, *"Gladly follow your husband, submitting to his leading. **Pray** for him, **encourage** him, **assist** him in* *embracing the vocations to which God calls him..."* for the glory of God and for the sake of His Kingdom here on earth.

Preparing Our Children
to Fulfill the Dominion Mandate

By Susan Eby

Video games were just in their infancy back when Dan and I were busy raising our young children. Birthday celebrations sometimes took place at the local pizza parlor where we watched the kids take turns gripping the wheel as they stared at the screen in intense concentration, fixated on the latest and greatest in kids' entertainment.

As I sat back watching them, it occurred to me at the time that one of those primitive video games might have been the best representation of what I felt that our goal was in our child-rearing responsibilities. Imagine a video game where a plane enters from the left side of the screen and travels across to the right, while all the time dozens of missiles are perpetually trying to attack it from the top and bottom. The goal, of course, is to navigate the plane from the left side to the right without getting hit. The goal was survival.

At the time, that was pretty much the picture of what I considered to be our moral and spiritual responsibility in raising our family: to protect our children from getting hit by the missiles. "Spiritual survival." If we could just get our children from the left side of the screen (their infancy) to the right side (their adulthood) by dodging constant attacks so that their faith remained intact by the time they arrived at adulthood, I would have felt like we'd succeeded.

Salvation, I believed, was our singular goal, the high point of our success, the point at which we would be able to breathe easy in the assurance that regardless of how bad the world was, at least our children would ultimately live in peace and joy forever in heaven.

But there was just one huge problem with that idea. It was man-centered, not God-centered.

It may have sounded lofty, but in reality, I had failed to consider Who and What they were being saved for, only how *they* would benefit from their salvation. My ultimate goal, inadvertently, was our children's eternal happiness. I wanted them to know the joy of forgiveness. A home in heaven. Answered prayers. Needs met. Miraculous healing. Deliverances. Successful marriages. Happy homes. Lots of great 'perks.'

Frankly, it just never really occurred to me that leading them to repentance and faith in Christ Jesus, as essential as it was, was not primarily for *their* benefit, but for *God's*– to equip them and send them on mission in God's great plan and purpose. In truth, salvation was the starting point at which they would spend the rest of their lives learning how to live out that faith in every area of life for the glory of God and the advancement of His Kingdom right here on the earth. And therefore, in a sense, our greater responsibility as parents training our children spiritually was just beginning at that point.

This reality hit in one very impacting moment when our children were attending a Christian school, and Dan and I sat listening to a guest speaker, Dennis Peacock, at a parent-teacher meeting.

"What if Jesus *doesn't* come back in your children's generation," the speaker started out challenging us. "What if things get worse than they are now? What if morality declines and the economy collapses? What if political systems fall apart? What if things get so bad that the world runs out of experiments and starts looking to Christians for real answers? *What are you preparing your children for?* Are you preparing them to have Godly answers in a culture that's falling apart?"

Though I'd been a Christian for a long, long time, in that moment I was jolted. Being "saved," I realized, means much, much more than merely a one-time verbal profession of believing in God so we can go to heaven. It involves a life committed to obeying the comprehensive nature of God's Word, expressed in the Bible, which has something to say about every aspect of life and living, with no exceptions. Our "confession" is our belief system, and it applies to every part of our lives. *What* do we believe about God?

Ever since that parent/teacher meeting, there's been a passion to learn how to apply God's Truth to all aspects of life for the glory of God and His Kingdom on the earth. What does God, through the Bible, say about work? About running a business? About education? About socialism, science, art, music, dance? About a woman's character, behavior, and role? About taxes, politics and government, health-care and charity? About relationships, money, family, institutions, marriage, divorce, health, care of our bodies, how we should dress?

That parent/teacher meeting took place more than 30 years ago, and sure enough, things have gotten drastically worse. If being saved 'so that we can go to heaven when we die' was really the answer for our culture, then why hasn't it had a better affect than we've seen over the last 30 years?

I really believe that it's because in raising our children, the church at large has been too self-focused, even in understanding the role of evangelism. This generation has failed to properly train our Christian young people in what

R.J. Rushdoony called their "dominion mandate." Genesis 1:28 is the command for man to *"be fruitful and multiply and fill the earth and subdue it, and have dominion over... every living thing that moves on the earth."*

To "subdue" is to tame, or to conquer. To "have dominion" is to govern God's creation as vice-regents of the Creator. He repeated the mandate to Noah after the flood, and repeated it again to the exiles of Israel when they were in Babylon. The dominion mandate is the application of our Christ-centered faith to all of life, thereby producing a true positive influence around us for the glory of God.

R.J.Rushdoony wrote:

> *"The center of our faith is not ourselves, but Christ and His Kingdom. Our salvation therefore is not the end of Christ's work, but its starting-point in our restoration into His household and calling. Calvin was right: our whole life must be our endeavor to fulfill His calling. Christ is the foundation, not we ourselves."*

Our parental responsibility is so much more than just waiting for that verbal profession of faith from our children, though that's important. It involves training them to apprehend the mission and call of God's dominion mandate, for the sake of the Kingdom of God and His glory. It's His Story after all, not ours.

This is no small feat in the midst of constant attacks that seek to perpetually dismantle the truths of God's commands! We are called by God to shape our children into deadly arrows in the midst of this warfare. And yet, it's not complicated.

God's Law is the Source of Freedom

Just a few weeks ago, Dan and I were at our annual regional work conference where scores of owners and managers of vacation rental businesses like ours can network and hear presentations on all aspects of successfully running our businesses. One of our sons is a very successful graphics designer, and although he does design work for us, he doesn't work in our business. He's a great public speaker, though, and in the past, he has given some presentations at these conference on ideas like successfully branding your business.

He wasn't at this recent conference, however, when a non-Christian business owner who had heard him in the past– as well as having contact with him over design ideas– asked if he could talk to me to find out how it was we had prepared our son so successfully to find his life's work.

At first, I didn't know what to say because there didn't seem to be much to tell. In situations like these, we tend to overthink the process when actually, it's not ours to strive over. God's Law guides us, and it's not as complex as we sometimes make it to be. His Law is very much like a railroad track. As long as we adhere to the track, there is incredible freedom to explore so many amazing places. But if we should ever deviate from the track, chaos and destruction are guaranteed. R.J. Rushdoony wrote:

> *"Disobedience begins with the illusion that God's Covenant Law is a restraint upon a people's freedom, rather than the ground of it."*

There were many avenues– many tracks– that our son *could* have taken in his career choices that we would have encouraged and blessed. At the same time, there were some that we would *not* have agreed to, if they conflicted with our Christian faith and obedience to Christ and His

Law. God has gifted and equipped each of our children to fulfill their individual God-given purposes on the earth. Our job is to encourage them each to follow their gifting appropriately, in compliance to God's Law.

Our children have tremendous freedom to follow their particular gifts and talents as they honor God in pursuit of their particular callings, and within that freedom, God is faithful to sovereignly direct them into His Will in their lives.

Consequently, preparing our children for their vocation does not begin with "what do we **do**," but with "what do we **believe**" about God, about man, and about which of these has the final word–the ultimate authority– over *every* issue that mankind must deal with in this current culture in which we are living.

What we believe about these three fundamental ideas forms our worldview– that lens of faith through which we view everything– and will determine whether our children will be equipped to exercise the mandate God commanded for His glory on this earth– or whether they will merely survive spiritually.

Who is God?

If I were to tell my neighbor that "God" is the answer for his every struggle, I may be surprised to find that he might actually agree. Truthfully, there are not a lot of individuals in America who don't believe in "God," just as there are few, if any, who don't have faith. As we've already noted, in our culture there is no lack of faith– but, as R.J. Rushdoony said, most of it is false.

In the same way, the majority of American individuals would probably say they believe in God, but what most of them believe *about* God– even within many evangelical churches–

is likewise false. To some, 'God' might be Allah. Or Buddha. Or Santa Claus. Or a big black Mama called Papa. Oprah Winfrey says she believes in God, and she believes *we* are Him. Well, actually, she believes we are *Her.* Does Oprah believe that 'God' is the answer to her problems? Yes, of course she does. And she believes that she herself is that answer.

This is not new, of course. As though it were this time and this culture, Paul warned the men of Athens that, *"being God's offspring, we ought not to think that the divine being is...formed by the imagination of man"* (Acts 17:29) and yet that's exactly what's happening in America today. America's concept of God is an imaginary conglomeration of everything we *want* Him to be.

Charles Spurgeon once wrote:

> *"Whatever a man depends upon, whatever rules his mind, whatever governs his affections, whatever is the chief object of his delight, is his god."*

The postmodern Christian's concept of God bears this out. In a culture where humanism is the dominant philosophy, "man" is the center of what that individual perceives God to be.

But there is only one true God. There are not "many" Gods. Jesus Christ is not just a viable option at the table of pluralism. There are not multiple paths, all leading to the same end. There is only one God, and only one way to Him, through His Son Jesus Christ.

"There is none else beside Him," says Deuteronomy 4:35

"I am the Lord, there is none else," II Samuel 7:22

"There is one God; and there is none other," Mark 12:32

As women, and especially as mothers, we have a wonderful advantage to help grasp who God is. In Joni Eareckson Tada's book, *Heaven: Your Real Home,* she refers to earth as "heaven's womb."

Now that's a concept we can understand! There are not many pictures more clear than that of a child growing in utero that can help us comprehend Who God is, and who we are. The fetus, still in the process of being shaped, formed, and prepared for his entrance into the world, is *in* the world, *surrounded* by the world, and in fact is *part* of the world– but he has not yet been released into it.

As that fetus is in the process of being formed for life that is so much more than the limited, dark confines of the womb, so we too who are in the world are in the process of being shaped and formed for a Kingdom that is far greater than just this earthly life.
Even now, we are part of the Kingdom of God, though we have not been released into the fullness of it yet.

Everything that we do on earth is intrinsically connected to that greater Kingdom that is so much more than this world, and yet touches every part of it. We are being shaped and formed for what's ahead! That's why we are here. Everything we do on earth counts for eternity, and everything your child does on earth counts for eternity, including his vocation and how he lives it out.

Who is man?

Now let's take a good, hard look at who man is. More specifically, let's look at the raw material that you have been given to work with in your role as a mother.

Our children do not begin life with a neutral moral compass, just a blank slate waiting to be written upon. If only parenting were that easy! The truth is that from the very start, every child has experienced the continual pull of a sin nature wanting to deny others and please himself– just like every one of the rest of us have. The parents' job is to constantly turn him away from the focus on himself, to the God-centered focus of a pleasant, hardworking, productive Kingdom adult, exercising the Dominion Mandate for the glory of God.

It's a big job. And if this task seems impossible to accomplish, well, that's because it *is*, if we're trying to do it in our own wisdom and ability. Parenting is the toughest, most humbling job we'll likely ever encounter. At the same time, it's absolutely the greatest joy and privilege that we will ever be called to accomplish, but it's totally impossible, if we think we can do it on our own, absent of God's enabling grace.

Impossible situations– those times when we just can't do it, when we're driven beyond our own ability, forced to cry out to God for His intervention– seem to be the primary tools He uses to forge us into the intensely God-focused, truly Theo-centric Kingdom participants we're called to be.

Your calling as a mother must be God-centered, not man-centered. Jesus calls us to humble ourselves– of all things– like little children. In Matthew 18 Jesus affirmed them, saying, *"Let the little children come to me and do not hinder them, for to such belongs the kingdom of heaven."* Think about it–the humble, the helpless, the dependent, the weak, the imperfect. *These* are what demonstrate the Kingdom of Heaven?

Immediately after, he was approached by the rich young man who boasted in his own self-righteous ability to keep God's law, yet still could not bring himself to separate from his riches– the product of his own sufficiency, his greatest distraction. After the young man walked away sorrowful,

Jesus reminded his disciples that it's easier for a camel to go through the eye of a needle than for a rich man to part with his riches and enter the Kingdom of God. To the disciples, it seemed impossible for *anybody* to be saved, but Jesus said, *"With man* [i.e. with man-centered faith]*, this is impossible, but with God* [i.e. with God-centered Faith] ***all things are possible."***

Like it was for that rich young man, spiritual pride is a far too common chink in our armor. We know the absolute necessity of God's Law, and yet if and when we slide into the pride of believing we have the ability within ourselves to keep God's Law, we *will* be humbled.

The greatest gift you can give your children is this clear picture of who God is, and who man is.

The task that He has given mothers is seemingly "impossible," and yet the call of God on your life as a mother is the most amazing thing you will ever know. You are called, by God's grace, to humbly understand who you are– and who your children are– as you find God's amazing enabling strength and grace day by day in the call of God on your life to accomplish the impossible. And with God, *all* things are possible.

Who is in Control?

When our kids were very young, our daughter came running into the kitchen one day, sobbing, "The boys keep calling me 'Constitution!' *Make them stop!"*

Our Constitution– the set of rules that govern us– was the boys' way of communicating intense frustration over a bossy little sister who was always trying to have the last word in correcting them. And if you're a mother, I can pretty much guarantee you've also heard your kids squabbling just like this until one of them, exasperated, finally shouts, "Who made *you* the boss!?" It's the ultimate sibling insult. Am I right?

It's also pretty much the oldest trick in the book. When Joseph's brothers were stirred with jealousy after he dreamed that their sheaves of wheat bowed down to his sheaf, they angrily scoffed, "So *you're* going to rule over *us*!?" (Genesis 37:8.)

And even Moses had his own frustrations when his siblings, Aaron and Miriam, accused him with, "Has the Lord spoken only through *you*? Hasn't he spoken through *us* too?" (Numbers 12:1,2.) They fell headlong into the complaints of the Israelites who accused Moses with, "Who made *you* a judge over us!?" (Exodus 2:14.)

It's classic. There always has been, and always will be, conflict over who has the last word, and it doesn't stop with siblings or with children. In our current culture, there's intense conflict over social and moral issues as one side accuses the other of legislating morality. "Who are *you* to tell me how to live my life?"

So who *can* tell us how to live our lives? Who *does* have the last word? *Who* has the authority to dictate how we wrestle through these issues? Right now, and historically, a very humanistic culture is pressing us to believe that whatever the individual decides is right for his own life is okay, because each man has ultimate authority over his own self. But *does* he?

Like it or not, man does not have the final say, even over his own life or over the issues taking place in his own life. There is a higher authority that mankind must submit to, whether or not the individual wants to accept it. Colossians 1:16, one of my favorite verses ever– says:

"By Him all things were created in heaven and on earth, visible and invisible, whether thrones or dominions or rulers or authorities. All things were created through Him and for Him."

By virtue of the fact that God created the world and is Sovereign over every square inch of it, He alone holds the final authority– has the last word– on every issue. Period. Game over.

After His resurrection, and before He ascended up into heaven, the last thing Jesus said was, *"All authority in heaven and on earth has been given to me. Go therefore and make disciples of all nations..."* (Matthew 28:18.) The world He left was still deep in sin and corruption, and yet still, His last instruction was a reminder of the declaration that He held Sovereign authority over all.

Abraham Kuyper once wrote:

"There is not a square inch in the whole domain of our human existence over which Christ, who is Sovereign over all, does not cry, Mine!"

Similarly, C.S.Lewis wrote:

"There is no neutral ground in the universe: every square inch, every split second, is claimed by God and counterclaimed by Satan."

Like never before in our lifetime, in today's American culture, the clash of two opposing world-views is more evident than ever: an anthropocentric [i.e.man- centered] worldview is not only in conflict with, but is waging all-out warfare against a comprehensive Theocentric [i.e. God- centered] worldview. It's the warfare of Humanism against the Christian belief system- the clash of opposing world views, the war over which one has "the last word–" man, or God.

This is what your children must understand unquestionably: Ephesians 1:20-21 says:

> "...[God] raised [Christ] from the dead and seated him at his right hand in the heavenly places, far above all rule and authority and power and dominion, and above every name that is named, not only in this age, but also in the one to come..."

No matter what the world is trying to force or coerce you into believing, man does not have the final word. Jesus Christ does. He alone is our standard of measuring what is right and what is wrong. Therefore, killing babies is not okay. Same sex marriage is not okay. Adultery is not okay. Broken marriage is not okay. Euthanasia is not okay. Murder is not okay. Pretending you are a different sex is not okay. Anything that offends God and challenges His Sovereign authority is not okay.

As long as we're on the earth, we are subject to multiple earthly authorities, always under God– husbands, parents, teachers, civil leaders. But if and when any of these should violate God's higher authority, we have no choice but to obey God rather than man.

As individuals, there is only one legitimate form of control that we are called– in fact commanded– to practice. Galatians 5:22 speaks of the virtuous aspect of "control" that can only come from the Holy Spirit's presence in our lives: self-control. It's the ability to control our own selves, not arbitrarily, but by the power of the Holy Spirit, according to the standards and precepts set out for us in the Bible.

It's learning to be God-centered in the way in which we measure all of life, falling back on His wisdom to guide us even when we can't see how it will turn out in the end. It's trusting that He knows what He is doing, and submitting ourselves to the Holy Spirit controlling our thoughts, acts, and deeds according to what pleases Him. Only God Himself holds the right to complete control.

Neither are we ever called to ultimately control anyone other than ourselves. That's when it becomes sin. Our goal as mothers is to teach our children to be self-controlled individuals, not to continually control them. *"God gave us a spirit not of fear, but of power and love and self-control,"* 2 Tim. 1:7. To do that, we must learn when to let go. Watch me do it. Then do it with me. Then I'll watch you do it. Then you do it.

The first lesson that our children will ever comprehend in self-control is learned by watching us. Yikes! Now that's convicting! What they see in us is their first and loudest teacher.

A mother's job is to help her children to learn self-control by providing just enough external controls to guide them, applying Biblical truths and principles to their lives, empowered by the Holy Spirit. (Proverbs 22:6.) The goal in preparing your children for their callings is to produce self-controlled individuals. The more internal self-control the child can exercise, the less external control is necessary. The hardest part for parents is to know when to let go of the external controls.

Conclusion

There's an inscription on the Pilgrim Mother's monument in Plymouth, Massachusetts that reads:
   "They brought up their families in sturdy virtue and a living faith in God, without which nations perish."

That's your task, mothers.

Your vocation is to prepare faithful children who will embrace *their* vocations to the glory of God, thereby fulfilling the dominion mandate that they were commanded to exercise. Without it, our nation will perish.

Again, "vocation" was beautifully defined by Steven Garber as:

> *"the wholeness of life, the range of relationships and responsibilities. Work, yes, but also families, and neighbors, and citizenship... that to which I am called as a human being, living my life before the face of God."*

We must never forget the goal, especially in the seeming drudgery of working this out day to day in continual acts of serving others.

G.K. Chesterton once wrote:

> *"How can it be a large career to tell other people's children about the Rule of Three, and a small career to tell one's own children about the universe? How can it be broad to be the same thing to everyone, and narrow to be everything to someone? No. A woman's function is laborious, but because it is gigantic, not because it is minute. I will pity Mrs. Jones for the hugeness of her task; I will never pity her for it's smallness."*

I recently read a book written by the astronaut Scott Kelly, chronicling the year he spent living in the International Space Station, 250 miles away from earth, zipping along at 17,500 mph. His mission was dangerous and amazing as he participated in the pursuit of man not only traveling into space, but learning to live in space. His mission was gigantic– and yet it was worked out largely in the day to day chores and seemingly boring routines of fixing broken equipment, making sure the toilet was working, watering flowers he was growing in space, experimenting with mice, growing lettuce to eat, preparing meals in an zero-gravity environment.

No matter how rote or how seemingly insignificant his routine seemed to be at the time, he never lost sight of the grander mission. And so it is with your call as a mother. Much of the working out of your vocation is made up of seemingly insignificant routine, and most of it is accomplished by serving others. But you must never lose sight of the call and mission! You are called by God to accomplish a huge and significant mission for the glory of God and the advancement of His Kingdom on the earth. Without it, nations perish. And you do it through serving.

As Charles Surgeon once addressed mothers:

> *"You are as much serving God in looking after your own children, training them up in God's fear, minding the house, and making your household a church for God as you would be if you had been called to lead an army to battle for the Lord of Hosts."*

Your call as mothers is to raise children who will be deadly arrows in the battle that's currently being waged against God and His ultimate authority, and they will do it by fulfilling their God-given dominion mandate. But believe me, it's not a video game– it's very, very real.

Conclusion

By Joseph M. Graham

I never had the pleasure of meeting R. J. Rushdoony, but I have gotten to meet his son, Mark, who is as gracious and humble of a man that I have ever met. My wife and I early on in our marriage decided to put our family near and close to as many of the great and inspirational Christian teachers as feasible. While many great teachers left us written records, which we utilize, it is a special grace to be able to sit across from a man, fellowship and commune with him.

The PNW Christian Reconstruction Symposiums and other events are great opportunities to meet and talk with these teachers and get to know them over a meal. My family and the other hosts are all extremely grateful for Mr. Rushdoony's particular contribution to this event.

There are many small aspects of an event that are missed by only reviewing the material that we covered. As a reader, you don't see the flood of children running through the grass laughing and tripping over each other. You miss out on in-depth conversations with adults and older children over a crackling campfire under cloud scattered skies. There are no mosquitos to contend with when you sit reading, nor dishwashing rotations to manage. You didn't get to stand and sing with us before we listened to a keynote speaker nor judge the children's note-taking contest.

In reality, the heart of the event that makes it stick in your mind comes from the relationships and memories that we experience in the mild summer mountain valley. Those connections and experiences between speakers, adults, and children will be what stays with me the most after our event.

The work of Christian Reconstruction is still early in its development. Every subject under God's sun must be subdued to the Lordship of Christ. The children of God have a big task ahead of themselves. The old saying about eating an elephant one piece at a time certainly applies. This event was meant to be a beginning for the many future subjects that we hope to address.

We will never be able to stray too far without constantly remembering the foundations behind our worldview. Over time we tend to forget, and because there will always be others that need to be reminded about the extent and far-reaching implications of the treasures of wisdom and knowledge.

The core ideas behind Christian Reconstruction have implications across the full breadth of human experiences. Believers in the future will advance Biblical principles into arenas and concepts beyond our imagination!

The Biblical presuppositional view drastically affects our view of God, and especially man. Fallible man has many limitations which are only righted by the perfect and right word of God. We can't forget this.

The full impact of the postmillennial eschatology is broad and deep. Thinking that we are still early in church history is both fantastic and frightening. These contemplations dramatically color our view of the past and the future. Each core concept necessarily touches on the others, and paints a picture for Christians of an incredible scope of work to be done.

We certainly cannot ever expect to escape the necessity for business and the fundamental entity that gives it its direction, purpose, and power– the family. The dominion mandate continues, and the expectation that Adam should expand the Lordship of Christ through service guarantees that there will be plenty of opportunities for businesses to thrive. Maintaining our vision for a future of generational influence means that the pioneers must lay strong foundations upon which their progeny can build.

Since dominion is a family task, we will need exceptionally dedicated, humble, and well-suited helpers. The completion of man's duties can only be fulfilled through a unity between husbands and wives. This fundamental relationship must always be strengthened and protected. We must never forget that the transmission of Christian beliefs and ethics is also essential for the health of the family.

Come be a part of a future symposium or event and experience the blessings of applying God's Word to every area of life. Visit us at reconstructionlife.com!

We've only started to decipher the intricate tapestry the Lord has given us concerning our task. There is much more to address and much more to learn. We heartily give thanks, in the name of our Lord Jesus Christ, to God the Father for the privilege of these opportunities.

Symposium on Christian Reconstruction